MY FATHER'S BUSINESS

MESSIAH IN THE MARKETPLACE

TORRANCE MACKINS JR

CONTENTS

Welcome Note from the Author v

Introduction. Why Lead Like Jesus? vii

Chapter 1. Identity First: "This Is My Beloved Son" 1

Chapter 2. Consistency of Message: "The Kingdom of God" 17

Chapter 3. Symbols, Stories, and Signature Moves (Your Visual & Experiential Brand) 33

Chapter 4. Storytelling Mastery: The Power of Parables . . 49

Chapter 5. Word of Mouth: Go and Tell 65

Chapter 6. Building a Core Team: The Twelve 82

Chapter 7. Servant Leadership: Washing Feet 99

Chapter 8. Emotional Intelligence: Weeping Over Jerusalem 117

Chapter 9. Handling Opposition: Engaging Pharisees and Critics 136

Chapter 10. Strategic Timing: "My Hour Has Not Yet Come" 152

Chapter 11. The Power of Storytelling: Parables as Marketing 169
Chapter 12. Excellence in Execution: Feeding the Five Thousand 187
Chapter 13. Branding Through Identity: "I Am" Statements of Jesus....................203
Chapter 14. Building Loyalty: Discipleship as Customer Retention 220
Chapter 15. Legacy and Succession: The Great Commission....................238
Chapter 16. Conclusion: Leading Like Jesus in the Marketplace 256

Epilogue. The Call to Lead Like Jesus....................275
Devotional Prayer 279

Welcome Note from the Author

Dear Reader,

First, let me say how grateful I am that you picked up this book. I don't believe it's by accident that you're holding it in your hands right now. Whether you're a business owner, entrepreneur, leader, or simply someone who desires to influence others with integrity and purpose, this book was written with you in mind.

I've spent years studying the principles of leadership, branding, and marketing. Yet, in my own journey, I found that the greatest leader who ever lived—Jesus Christ—provided a model unlike any other. His clarity of identity, His wisdom in timing, His ability to connect through story, His excellence in execution, His loyalty to those He led, and His preparation for legacy form a blueprint that is as relevant in today's marketplace as it was two thousand years ago.

My heart in writing this book is not only to share strategies but also to point you to the Source. Jesus is more than a leadership model—He is Savior and Lord. If you don't yet know Him personally, I hope the pages ahead will stir something deeper in you. If you already follow Him, my prayer is that these lessons will sharpen your leadership and expand your influence.

So, whether you are flipping through these pages in search of practical tools or eternal truths, I welcome you to this journey. Let's learn together what it truly means to lead like Jesus—in life, in business, and in legacy.

With gratitude and expectation,

Torrance Mackins Jr.

INTRODUCTION

Why Lead Like Jesus?

Every generation faces the same challenges in leadership: how do we inspire trust, build loyalty, communicate clearly, and leave a legacy? For centuries, experts have offered models of leadership, management, branding, and marketing. Yet, no leader has left a greater impact on history than Jesus Christ.

Though He never held political office, commanded an army, or ran a corporation, His influence has shaped nations, inspired movements, and transformed lives for over two thousand years. He did this not by following the trends of His time but by embodying eternal values: clarity of identity, wisdom in timing, the power of story, excellence in execution, loyalty through relationship, and legacy through succession.

This book explores how the principles Jesus lived out in the Gospels—Matthew, Mark, Luke, and John—are not only spiritual truths but also practical strategies for branding, marketing, and selling in today's world. You will discover that the way Jesus built His movement has direct application for how you can build your business, organization, or personal brand with integrity and purpose.

Why Jesus' Leadership Matters in the Marketplace

In the modern marketplace, leaders are under pressure to perform, compete, and deliver results. Too often, this leads to shortcuts, compromise, or burnout. But when we look to Jesus, we see a leader who never compromised His values, never lost His focus, and never failed to deliver on His mission.

- He knew His identity and communicated it with boldness.
- He understood timing and moved with precision.
- He used stories to connect with ordinary people.
- He executed His mission with excellence that multiplied impact.
- He built loyalty by investing deeply in people.
- He ensured His legacy by preparing others to carry the mission forward.

What He modeled in ministry is what we desperately need in business and leadership today.

This Book's Purpose

This book is written for leaders, entrepreneurs, business owners, and anyone who desires to influence others with integrity and impact. It is not about using Jesus as a marketing gimmick—it is about learning from His life as the greatest leader who ever lived.

By walking through His principles in detail, you will gain:

- Clarity on how to define and communicate your identity.
- Wisdom on discerning timing for decisions and opportunities.
- Skill in using storytelling to move hearts and minds.
- Discipline to execute with excellence in every detail.
- Strategies for building loyalty that endures.
- Insight on preparing for legacy and succession.

But beyond strategies, you will encounter a Person. Jesus Christ is not only a model of leadership—He is the Savior of the world.

A Personal Invitation

As you read this book, you may be approaching Jesus primarily as a leader and example. That is a good place to begin. But Jesus is more than an example—He is Lord and Savior. His leadership principles are powerful, but His greatest gift is salvation.

The Bible says in Romans 10:9, "If you declare with your mouth, 'Jesus is Lord,' and believe in your heart that God raised him from the dead, you will be saved." This is more than a concept—it is an invitation. Jesus died on the cross for your sins, rose from the dead in victory, and offers you eternal life.

If you have never accepted Him as your Savior, you can do so right now with a simple but sincere prayer:

Prayer of Salvation

Lord Jesus, I come to You today knowing that I am a sinner in need of a Savior. I believe You died on the cross for my sins and rose again in victory. Today, I confess You as Lord of my life. Forgive me, cleanse me, and make me new. I give You my heart, my life, and my future. From this day forward, I choose to follow You. Thank You for saving me. In Jesus' name, Amen.

If you prayed that prayer sincerely, the Bible declares that you are now a child of God. This is the greatest decision you will ever make. As you journey through this book, you will not only discover how to lead like Jesus in the marketplace—you will walk with Him as your Savior, Friend, and Lord.

Welcome to a new life of purpose, freedom, and leadership that endures.

CHAPTER 1

Identity First: "This Is My Beloved Son"

The Principle — Why Identity Precedes Activity

When we talk about branding, marketing, and selling, most people immediately think about action: running campaigns, closing deals, building websites, creating content, or pitching to clients. The modern business landscape reinforces this mindset. Everywhere you turn, experts are shouting: "Do more, post more, launch faster, hustle harder!" But when we look at the life of Jesus, we find a strikingly different order of priorities. Jesus didn't start His public ministry with action. He started with identity.

Before He healed the sick, multiplied loaves, or preached the Sermon on the Mount, He was baptized in the Jordan River by John. And in that moment, heaven opened, and the Father declared: "This is my beloved Son, in whom I am well pleased" (Matthew 3:17). That declaration set the stage for everything that would follow. It was not a motivational speech, not a strategy outline, not a "five-year plan." It was an affirmation of identity.

Why does this matter? Because activity without identity leads to confusion, burnout, and instability. If you start with activity, you may achieve temporary results, but you'll lack a foundation. If you start with identity, every action flows with clarity, focus, and long-term impact.

Identity as the Root of Influence

Think of identity like the roots of a tree. Roots are invisible to the eye, but they provide strength, nourishment, and stability. If the root system is shallow, the tree cannot stand against storms, and it cannot bear much fruit. But if the roots are deep, the tree can grow tall, weather harsh conditions, and provide shade and sustenance for generations.

Your personal or business brand works the same way. Logos, slogans, social media posts, and sales strategies are the visible branches and leaves. But the hidden root—the part no one sees—is identity. Who you are. What you stand for. Why you exist. If your root is strong, your brand can survive shifting markets, competitive pressures, and cultural changes. If your root is weak, you may grow fast, but you won't last.

The Fragility of Performance-Based Identity

Many entrepreneurs and professionals make the mistake of tying identity to performance. If sales are high, they feel confident. If likes and followers increase, they feel validated. If recognition comes, they feel secure. But when sales dip, engagement slows, or recognition fades, their sense of worth collapses. They ride a rollercoaster of highs and lows because their identity is tethered to external outcomes.

Jesus modeled something radically different. His identity was affirmed before He had performed any miracles or preached any sermons. The Father's declaration—"This is my beloved Son"—was not based on activity but on relationship. This shows us that true identity is not earned; it is received.

For business leaders, this is freeing. You are not defined by yesterday's results or today's market conditions. You are defined by the core truth of who you are and the mission you've embraced. When your identity is anchored in that, you can weather the fluctuations of business life without losing your sense of self.

Identity Clarifies Purpose

Another reason identity must come first is that it clarifies purpose. When you know who you are, you know what you are called to do. When you're unclear about identity, you end up chasing every opportunity, mimicking competitors, or diluting your message in an attempt to please everyone.

Consider a simple example: imagine two fitness trainers. One says, "I help anyone who wants to get in shape." The other says, "I help busy professionals over 40 regain their energy and strength through efficient 30-minute workouts." Which trainer do you trust more? The second, because their identity is clear. They know who they serve, what they do, and why it matters.

Identity eliminates confusion. It sets boundaries. It helps you say "no" to opportunities that look good but don't align with your purpose. Jesus demonstrated this when He refused to stay in one town despite pressure from crowds, saying, "I must proclaim the good news to other towns also, because that is why I was sent" (Luke 4:43). His identity defined His mission, and His mission dictated His actions.

Identity Produces Confidence

Confidence in business and leadership is not bravado—it's alignment. When you know who you are, you don't need to prove yourself. Jesus didn't scramble to validate His identity when the enemy challenged Him in the wilderness with the words, "If you are the Son of God..." (Luke 4:3). He simply stood on the truth already spoken over Him.

Likewise, when your brand identity is clear, you won't constantly compare yourself to competitors. You won't feel threatened by someone else's success. Instead, you can celebrate others while staying rooted in your lane. Confidence comes not from outworking everyone else, but from knowing and owning who you are.

Building an Identity-First Brand

So how do you practically build a brand that starts with identity? Begin by asking and answering four foundational questions:

1. Who am I? What are the values, beliefs, and strengths that define me?
2. Who do I serve? Who is my ideal audience or client?
3. What transformation do I bring? How is life different after someone works with me?
4. Why do I exist? What is my deeper mission beyond profit?

When you answer these questions, you create what I call your Identity Compass. This compass guides your decisions, filters your opportunities, and shapes your strategies.

For example, if your identity is "I help small business owners create financial freedom through smart real estate decisions," then every product, service, and piece of content you create should reinforce that truth. If a partnership opportunity comes along that doesn't align, you can confidently decline it, knowing it doesn't fit your compass.

Conclusion to the Principle

The principle is clear: identity must come before activity. Just as Jesus was affirmed as the beloved Son before beginning His ministry, you must establish your identity before diving into action. Activity without identity is noise. Identity before activity is clarity.

When your identity is rooted deeply—like the roots of a tree—you will not only grow but endure. You won't be shaken by storms, distracted by trends, or consumed by comparison. Instead, you will move with focus, confidence, and resilience, building a brand that is not just successful but sustainable.

Biblical Insight — Jesus' Identity in the Gospels

When we study the Gospels carefully, we see a pattern emerge: before Jesus did, He was. His identity was always the foundation of His mission. The evangelists—Matthew, Mark, Luke, and John—don't simply record His miracles or teachings; they consistently anchor His authority, His actions, and His ministry in the reality of who He is: the Son of God. Understanding this biblical pattern helps us grasp why identity is always the starting point for lasting influence.

The Baptismal Declaration

All three Synoptic Gospels (Matthew, Mark, Luke) record the baptism of Jesus. Each emphasizes the Father's affirmation. In Matthew 3:16–17, we read: "As soon as Jesus was baptized, he went up out of the water. At that moment heaven was opened, and he saw the Spirit of God descending like a dove and alighting on him. And a voice from heaven said, 'This is my Son, whom I love; with him I am well pleased.'"

This is a profound moment. Jesus hadn't performed a miracle yet. He hadn't preached. He hadn't trained disciples. Still, God the Father declared His pleasure in Him. Identity wasn't based on performance—it was declared by relationship. This tells us that identity is received, not earned.

Mark emphasizes the personal dimension: "You are my Son, whom I love; with you I am well pleased" (Mark 1:11). Luke echoes this, adding that Jesus was praying when the heavens opened (Luke 3:21–22). Together, the accounts show us identity affirmed publicly (for others to hear) and personally (for Jesus to internalize).

The Wilderness Temptation

Immediately after the baptism, Jesus was led into the wilderness by the Spirit. Here He faced temptation. Notice Satan's strategy: "If you are the Son of God..." (Luke 4:3, 9). The first thing challenged was not His power or authority—it was His identity.

Why? Because if the enemy could sow doubt about identity, he could derail the mission. Identity is the foundation of obedience. If you are not sure of who you are, you cannot walk confidently in what you are called to do.

Jesus responded not by proving Himself but by anchoring in Scripture. He quoted Deuteronomy three times, showing that His security wasn't in proving His identity through flashy displays but in trusting what God had already spoken. This reveals a timeless truth: when your identity is clear, you don't have to prove yourself—you simply live it.

The Mission Statement in Nazareth

After the wilderness, Jesus began His public ministry. In Luke 4:18–19, He read from Isaiah 61 in the synagogue: "The Spirit of the Lord is upon me, because He has anointed me to proclaim good news to the poor. He has sent me to proclaim freedom for the prisoners and recovery of sight for the blind, to set the oppressed free, to proclaim the year of the Lord's favor."

This was more than a reading—it was a declaration of identity and mission. By choosing this passage, Jesus was saying, "This is who I am. This is why I'm here." It functioned like a mission statement. From that point forward, everything He did aligned with this identity.

Identity Tested Throughout the Gospels

Throughout His ministry, Jesus' identity continued to be tested:

- The Pharisees questioned His authority: "By what authority are you doing these things?" (Matthew 21:23).

- People tried to redefine Him as merely a teacher, a prophet, or even a political leader.
- Even His disciples wrestled with His identity. Peter confessed, "You are the Messiah, the Son of the living God" (Matthew 16:16).

At critical moments, Jesus always returned to identity. He never allowed others to redefine Him. Even at His trial, when Pilate asked if He was King of the Jews, He responded firmly: "You say that I am" (John 18:37). He anchored His purpose in identity, even under pressure.

The Transfiguration and Final Affirmation

Later in His ministry, Jesus was again affirmed by the Father at the Transfiguration: "This is my Son, whom I love; with him I am well pleased. Listen to him!" (Matthew 17:5). This second declaration, in the presence of Peter, James, and John, reinforced His identity as the beloved Son. It showed that the Father's affirmation was not a one-time event but a continual reality.

By the time of His crucifixion, even a Roman centurion confessed: "Surely he was the Son of God!" (Mark 15:39). His identity remained central to His witness, even in death.

Lessons for Us

The Gospels make it clear: Jesus' identity was not peripheral—it was central. Without it, the miracles would be mere spectacles, the teachings mere wisdom sayings, the death of Christ a tragic end. But because He was the Son of God, everything He did carried eternal weight.

This has direct implications for us:

- Identity is always tested. Just as Satan questioned Jesus' identity, your identity will be questioned—by circumstances, by critics, and even by your own doubts.
- Identity fuels mission. Jesus' mission was clear because His identity was clear. If you lack clarity of identity, you'll lack clarity of mission.
- Identity must be reaffirmed. Just as Jesus was affirmed multiple times, we also need continual reminders of who we are. This can come through Scripture, mentors, and community.

Conclusion

The biblical narrative shows that identity is not just the starting point—it is the sustaining point. Jesus lived and ministered out of His identity as the Son of God. That's why He could resist temptation, stay focused on mission, and endure the cross.

For us, whether in life or business, the lesson is clear: if we don't root ourselves in identity, we will be tossed around by every challenge, trend, or opinion. But when identity is firm, everything else—strategy, activity, and impact—flows with purpose and power.

Business Application — Identity in Branding and Leadership

When we shift from the biblical narrative to the world of branding, marketing, and selling, the parallels become striking. Jesus modeled a principle that applies directly to entrepreneurs, leaders, and professionals today: identity precedes activity. Without identity, activity becomes noise. With identity, activity becomes impact. Let's unpack how this plays out in business and leadership.

Why Activity Without Identity Fails

Imagine a company that rushes to create social media posts, run ads, and design logos without first asking: Who are we? Who do we serve? Why do we exist? They may get short-term attention, but in the long term they will fail to stand out. Their brand will feel inconsistent because their actions are not anchored in a deeper truth.

This is the trap many fall into. They chase tactics without strategy. They try to sell without clarity. They mimic competitors instead of defining their own voice. The result? Confusion in the marketplace. Customers don't know who they are or what they stand for. In business, confusion kills sales.

The Power of Identity in Branding

Strong brands know exactly who they are. Consider Apple. Their identity isn't just about computers or phones; it's about creativity, simplicity, and challenging the status quo. That's why "Think Different" resonated so powerfully. Everything they create flows from that identity.

Nike is another example. Their identity is not shoes; it's empowerment. "Just Do It" speaks to determination, grit, and achievement. Their ads rarely talk about rubber soles—they talk about human spirit.

Closer to home, think about a small local business. A coffee shop that defines itself as "the place where community gathers" will make decisions differently than one that defines itself as "fast and affordable caffeine." Both may sell coffee, but their identity shapes their space, service, and marketing. One focuses on atmosphere and relationships; the other focuses on speed and price.

Your business needs this same clarity. Without it, you'll be pulled in every direction. With it, you'll stand firm, attract the right audience, and build loyalty.

Components of a Business Identity

Just as Jesus' identity was declared before His mission, your business identity must be clarified before your activities. Here are four components to define:

1. Who You Are
   What values, strengths, and beliefs define your brand? Are you about luxury or accessibility, innovation or tradition, speed or thoroughness?

2. Who You Serve
   Who is your audience? Be specific. Saying "everyone" means no one. Identify the age, lifestyle, challenges, and aspirations of the people you are uniquely positioned to serve.

3. What Transformation You Bring
   What change happens after someone interacts with your brand? Do they feel more confident, secure, empowered, informed, or inspired? Transformation is what sells—not just products.

4. Why You Exist
   Profit is a result, not a reason. What bigger mission drives your work? Maybe it's empowering families, supporting communities, or changing an industry standard. This deeper "why" gives meaning and motivates both you and your customers.

Case Study: Identity in Action

Let's say you're a real estate agent. Without identity, you may advertise: "I sell homes." So does every other agent. There's no differentiation. But if your identity is: "I help families transition into homes that fit their new chapter of life, making the process simple and stress-free," everything changes.

- Your marketing now focuses on life transitions—newlyweds, growing families, retirees downsizing.
- Your content addresses stress points: moving logistics, financial clarity, emotional decisions.
- Your brand tone becomes empathetic and reassuring, not just transactional.

The result? Clients feel seen, understood, and cared for. They don't just hire you to sell a house; they trust you to guide them through a life moment. That's the power of identity.

Identity as a Filter for Decisions

In business, opportunities constantly come your way: partnerships, new products, collaborations, marketing ideas. Without identity, you'll say "yes" to too much and end up stretched thin. Identity acts as a filter. You ask: Does this align with who we are and what we stand for? If not, you confidently say no.

Jesus modeled this. When the crowds wanted Him to stay, He said, "I must preach the good news of the kingdom of God to other towns also, because that is why I was sent" (Luke 4:43). He knew His mission, so He declined opportunities that didn't fit. Businesses must do the same.

Identity Builds Resilience

Markets change. Algorithms shift. Competitors rise. If your identity is based only on tactics, you'll crumble when circumstances shift. But when identity is anchored deeply, you can adapt tactics without losing direction.

For example, many businesses struggled when social media algorithms reduced reach. The ones that survived weren't those clinging to tactics but those with clear identities. They knew their mission and found new ways to live it out.

Identity makes you adaptable. You don't panic when trends change—you pivot while staying true to who you are.

Practical Steps

1. Write an Identity Statement: "I help [audience] overcome [problem] by [method] so they can [result]."
2. Define 3 Core Values. Write a one-sentence behavior for each. (E.g., "Excellence: we deliver beyond expectations every time.")

3. Create an Identity Filter: 5 questions to test every opportunity. (Does this align with our mission? Does it serve our audience? Does it reflect our values?)
4. Share your identity with your team, clients, and audience. Let people hold you accountable to it.

Conclusion to Business Application

Jesus began His ministry with identity, not activity. The same principle transforms businesses. When you know who you are, who you serve, the transformation you bring, and why you exist, everything else flows with clarity. Activity becomes purposeful. Marketing becomes consistent. Sales become natural.

Identity is your compass in a noisy world. Without it, you drift. With it, you stand firm, build trust, and create lasting impact.

CHAPTER 2

Consistency of Message: "The Kingdom of God"

The Principle — Why Consistency Builds Trust and Influence

In branding, marketing, and selling, one of the most overlooked truths is the power of consistency. You may have the best product, the most innovative service, or the flashiest advertising, but if your message is inconsistent, you will confuse your audience and weaken your impact. Confusion, in business, is deadly. People don't buy what they don't understand, and they don't trust what feels unstable.

When we look at Jesus, we see that His message was consistent from beginning to end. Whether He was teaching in a synagogue, preaching on a hillside, walking through villages, or having one-on-one conversations, His central theme remained the same: the Kingdom of God. Matthew records His earliest preaching: "Repent, for the kingdom of heaven has come near"

(Matthew 4:17). Mark echoes it: "The time has come… The kingdom of God has come near. Repent and believe the good news!" (Mark 1:15). Luke adds: "I must proclaim the good news of the kingdom of God to the other towns also, because that is why I was sent" (Luke 4:43).

This wasn't just a slogan—it was His identity translated into a message. Every parable, every miracle, every teaching was tied back to the Kingdom. He didn't scatter His words in a thousand directions. He returned again and again to the same truth, using different angles and stories to drive it home.

Why Consistency Matters

The human brain is wired to recognize and remember patterns. Repetition creates familiarity, and familiarity builds trust. This is why marketing experts talk about the "Rule of 7"—that people need to encounter a message multiple times before it sticks. Consistency in branding works the same way.

When your message is clear and repeated, people begin to associate you with that message. You "own" a space in their minds. When they think of fitness, they think of a trainer who always talks about strength over aesthetics. When they think of real estate, they think of an agent who always emphasizes peace of mind for families. When they think of leadership, they think of the voice who always connects leadership with service.

If, however, your message changes constantly—one week you talk about luxury, the next about affordability, the next about speed—your audience doesn't know who you are. They can't pin you down. And if they can't define you, they won't remember you.

The Dangers of Message Drift

Message drift is the slow slide away from clarity into chaos. It often happens when businesses chase trends. A competitor tries a new angle, so you mimic it. A customer makes a suggestion, so you shift your pitch. A consultant tells you the "new secret," so you adjust again. Over time, you lose sight of your original mission.

The result? Your message becomes fragmented. Different platforms tell different stories. Your emails emphasize one thing, your website another, your social media something else entirely. People get mixed signals. Instead of building trust, you erode it. Instead of growing influence, you shrink it.

Consistency doesn't mean stagnation. Jesus told dozens of parables, performed many types of miracles, and addressed different situations. But all of it pointed back to the same theme: the Kingdom. Consistency is about keeping the core message stable while expressing it in fresh, creative ways.

The Long-Term Power of Consistency

Building a brand is not about making noise—it's about making memory. You don't want people to say, "They're always saying something new." You want them to say, "They're always saying the same thing, in new ways." That's how you build reputation. That's how you become the trusted voice in your space.

Consistency also creates alignment inside your business. When your team knows the central message, they can communicate it with confidence. Your customer service team echoes it in how they treat clients. Your sales team echoes it in pitches. Your marketing team echoes it in campaigns. The more consistent the message, the stronger the culture.

Think of Coca-Cola. Their central message has been about happiness, joy, and refreshment for decades. The ads change. The slogans evolve. The visuals update. But the message is the same. That's why they remain one of the most recognized brands worldwide.

Bringing It Back to Jesus

Jesus never suffered from message drift. He didn't one day emphasize wealth, another day power, another day fame. He stayed rooted in the Kingdom. Even when people tried to pull Him into political debates or personal agendas, He returned to His message. "My kingdom is not of this world" (John 18:36). Consistency was His strength. It's why His words are remembered two millennia later.

For your business, this means defining your central message and refusing to drift. Ask yourself: If someone described me or my brand in one sentence, what would it be? If your message isn't that clear, you have work to do.

Conclusion

The principle is straightforward: consistency creates clarity, and clarity builds trust. If people don't know what you stand for, they won't remember you, and if they don't remember you, they won't buy from you.

Consistency doesn't mean boring repetition—it means hammering home the same truth in creative, fresh ways until it sticks. Just like Jesus proclaimed the Kingdom of God in parables, miracles, and sermons, your job is to find multiple ways to say the same thing until people finally see, hear, and believe it.

Biblical Insight — The Consistent Message of Jesus in the Gospels

When we read Matthew, Mark, Luke, and John, one theme emerges again and again: Jesus was consistent. His message never wavered. From His first recorded sermon to His post-resurrection conversations with His disciples, He pointed people toward one central reality: the Kingdom of God.

This consistency is more than a detail—it's a model. It shows us how Jesus built credibility, trust, and influence. The consistency of His message not only attracted crowds but also trained disciples, who later carried that same message to the ends of the earth.

Let's walk through how each Gospel emphasizes Jesus' consistent proclamation.

Matthew: "Repent, for the Kingdom of Heaven is at Hand"

Matthew records Jesus' first public message in Matthew 4:17: "From that time Jesus began to preach, saying, 'Repent, for the kingdom of heaven is at hand.'" Notice that Matthew doesn't say Jesus occasionally spoke about the Kingdom—he says this was the beginning of His consistent preaching.

The Sermon on the Mount (Matthew 5–7) is essentially a masterclass on Kingdom living. Jesus used contrast after contrast to show what the Kingdom looks like compared to earthly systems:

- "You have heard it said... but I say to you..."
- "Blessed are the poor in spirit, for theirs is the kingdom of heaven."
- "Seek first the kingdom of God and his righteousness..." (Matthew 6:33).

The Gospel of Matthew uses the phrase "kingdom of heaven" 32 times. It was the thread woven through Jesus' parables, His ethical teachings, and His miracles. The point is unmistakable: His message was not scattered. It was consistent.

Mark: "The Time Has Come"

Mark summarizes Jesus' ministry in one sweeping sentence: "The time has come... The kingdom of God has come near. Repent and believe the good news!" (Mark 1:15). That's it. Mark doesn't complicate things. He presents the message as urgent, simple, and focused.

Throughout Mark's Gospel, Jesus demonstrates the Kingdom through action. His miracles, healings, and authority over demons were not random acts of compassion only—they were signs that the Kingdom was breaking into the world. The message and the actions were aligned. He consistently backed up His words with demonstrations of power.

Even when He taught in parables, Mark notes: "He taught them many things by parables..." (Mark 4:2). The parables consistently pointed to Kingdom realities: seeds growing, mustard trees, hidden treasure, a net gathering fish. Different images, same theme.

Luke: "I Must Proclaim the Good News"

Luke captures Jesus' clarity in Luke 4:43: "But he said, 'I must proclaim the good news of the kingdom of God to the other towns also, because that is why I was sent.'" Here Jesus

Himself explains His mission. Preaching the Kingdom was not optional—it was essential. It was why He was sent.

Luke also highlights Jesus' parables of compassion—the Good Samaritan (Luke 10), the Prodigal Son (Luke 15), the Lost Sheep and Lost Coin (Luke 15). Each of these stories reflected the nature of the Kingdom: mercy, forgiveness, restoration, celebration.

In Luke 8:1, we read: "After this, Jesus traveled about from one town and village to another, proclaiming the good news of the kingdom of God. The Twelve were with him..." Luke makes it explicit: wherever Jesus went, the message remained the same. Different towns, different audiences, same Kingdom.

John: "My Kingdom Is Not of This World"

John's Gospel doesn't use the phrase "kingdom of God" as often as the Synoptics, but the concept is still central. When Jesus spoke to Nicodemus, He said, "Very truly I tell you, no one can see the kingdom of God unless they are born again" (John 3:3). His conversation about new birth was tied directly to entering the Kingdom.

Later, when interrogated by Pilate, Jesus declared: "My kingdom is not of this world" (John 18:36). Even under political pressure, even when His life was on the line, His message didn't shift. He didn't suddenly redefine His mission as political. He remained consistent: His Kingdom was spiritual, eternal, and unshakable.

Consistency in Parables and Miracles

It's important to note that Jesus used a variety of methods—stories, metaphors, miracles—but all pointed to the same central truth. For example:

- Parables: Seeds (growth of the Kingdom), treasure (value of the Kingdom), a banquet (invitation to the Kingdom).
- Miracles: Healing the blind (sight in the Kingdom), feeding the hungry (abundance in the Kingdom), casting out demons (freedom in the Kingdom).

Different expressions, one consistent message. This demonstrates a key principle: consistency doesn't mean monotony. Jesus didn't repeat the same sentence over and over. He repeated the same truth in new, engaging ways.

Why the Consistency Matters Biblically

So why did the Gospel writers highlight this so much? Because consistency proves authenticity. False teachers change their message depending on the audience. Manipulators shift their words to fit agendas. But Jesus spoke with authority and consistency. That's why crowds said, "He teaches as one who has authority, not as their teachers of the law" (Matthew 7:29).

Consistency also made the disciples effective. Because Jesus drilled the Kingdom message into them, they carried it forward with clarity. After His resurrection, Acts 1:3 says He appeared to them over 40 days "and spoke about the kingdom of God." Even after the cross, resurrection, and empty tomb, the message hadn't changed. That's how the movement spread so powerfully: everyone was aligned around one consistent truth.

Lessons from the Gospels

From a biblical standpoint, here's what we learn about consistency:

1. It's essential to mission. Jesus said preaching the Kingdom was why He was sent.
2. It's proven by repetition. The same theme surfaces across all Gospels, parables, and miracles.
3. It builds authority. Consistency distinguished Jesus from the religious leaders of His day.
4. It multiplies influence. The disciples carried the same consistent message worldwide.

Conclusion

The Gospels make it clear: Jesus' consistent message of the Kingdom was not accidental—it was central. He never drifted into side agendas. He never allowed others to redefine His mission. He stayed focused, and because of that, His words are remembered and repeated to this day.

For us, this is more than history. It's a blueprint. If we want to build influence that lasts, if we want our message to stick, we must follow Jesus' example: choose one central truth and repeat it consistently across everything we do.

Business Application — Consistency in Branding, Marketing, and Sales

If there is one thing that separates trusted brands from forgettable ones, it's consistency. Customers trust what they understand and distrust what confuses them. Inconsistent brands may get attention for a moment, but consistent brands build credibility for decades. Jesus modeled this in His ministry by relentlessly focusing on the Kingdom of God. For us, this principle becomes a practical roadmap for building influence and growing a sustainable business.

Why Consistency Builds Trust

Imagine meeting someone who introduces themselves with a different job title every week. One week they say they're a lawyer, the next week a teacher, then a musician, then an investor. How much trust would you place in their expertise? Probably very little.

This is exactly what happens when businesses constantly change their message. If one ad says, "We're the fastest option," another says, "We're the cheapest," and another says, "We're the most luxurious," the audience gets mixed signals. Customers think: Who are you, really? Confusion always kills conversion.

On the other hand, when a brand consistently communicates the same promise, people begin to associate that message with them. For example:

- FedEx: "When it absolutely, positively has to be there overnight."
- Volvo: Safety.
- Starbucks: A "third place" between home and work.

These companies have offered other things over the years, but their core message remained consistent. That's why people trust them.

Consistency Creates Memorability

Human memory is shaped by repetition. That's why slogans, jingles, and taglines are repeated endlessly in advertising. The more often people hear the same message, the more likely they are to remember it.

The same principle applies in content creation. If every blog post, video, or podcast episode you create highlights a different random theme, your audience will not know what to associate with you. But if every piece of content points back to your core message, eventually people will say, "That's the person who always talks about ___." That's how you occupy mental real estate.

Jesus did this masterfully. He didn't just say "Kingdom of God" once and move on. He wove it into parables, sermons, miracles, and even one-on-one conversations. The consistency made His teaching unforgettable. Businesses must do the same.

Consistency Across Platforms

Modern branding lives across multiple channels: websites, emails, social media, podcasts, printed materials, and in-person conversations. If your message is inconsistent across these platforms, you create friction for your audience.

Here's a common mistake: A company's website says they are premium and high-quality, but their social media posts focus on discounts and bargains. Their ads promise luxury, but their customer service communicates speed over care. Customers experience dissonance, and trust is eroded.

The fix is to create a Message Map. A message map has one headline statement (your central promise) supported by 3–5 pillars (key themes). Every platform uses the same headline and rotates through the pillars. That way, whether a customer finds you on Instagram, your website, or in a sales conversation, they hear the same message.

Consistency Builds Culture

Consistency isn't just external—it's internal. When your team knows the core message, they can embody it in their daily work.

Your marketing, sales, and customer service departments no longer operate in silos—they harmonize around one shared truth.

For example, if your brand promise is "We make financial planning simple for families," your marketing team should emphasize clarity, your sales team should highlight easy-to-understand solutions, and your customer service should simplify processes. When everyone echoes the same message, the culture strengthens, and customers notice.

Consistency Multiplies Sales

Sales is essentially about trust. People buy when they trust that you can deliver what you promise. Consistency accelerates that trust. When a prospect hears the same message across multiple touchpoints—your ads, your website, your sales call—they feel more confident that the promise is real.

Inconsistent messaging, however, creates doubt. If a prospect hears three different promises, they assume one (or all) of them might be untrue. Doubt kills deals. Consistency closes them.

Balancing Consistency and Freshness

One fear many entrepreneurs have is that consistency will make them sound repetitive or boring. But repetition is not the same as monotony. The key is to repeat the same truth in fresh ways.

Jesus told dozens of parables, but they all pointed to the Kingdom. Nike has used "Just Do It" for decades, but every campaign feels fresh because they highlight new athletes, stories, and cultural moments. You don't need a new message—you need new angles.

Practical Steps

1. Write Your Headline Message
   Summarize your brand promise in one sentence. (E.g., "We help families build wealth through smart real estate decisions.")
2. Define 3–5 Message Pillars
   These are supporting themes that reinforce your headline. (E.g., education, transparency, speed, service.)
3. Audit Your Platforms
   Review your website, social media, ads, proposals. Are they aligned around the same headline and pillars?
4. Train Your Team
   Share the message map with everyone in your organization. Role-play how it sounds in marketing, sales, and service conversations.
5. Rotate, Don't Replace
   Keep the core message the same, but rotate through pillars in content creation to keep things fresh.

Conclusion

Consistency of message is not optional—it's essential. In business, inconsistency creates confusion, and confusion kills trust. Jesus' ministry shows us that a clear, consistent message not only builds credibility but also multiplies influence.

If you want people to remember you, repeat your core message. If you want people to trust you, align your actions and words around that message. If you want your influence to last, resist message drift and stay anchored.

Like Jesus, you don't need a thousand different messages. You need one truth expressed consistently and creatively until it becomes unforgettable.

CHAPTER 3

Symbols, Stories, and Signature Moves (Your Visual & Experiential Brand)

The Principle — Why Symbols and Experiences Make a Brand Memorable

When people think about branding, they often picture logos, color palettes, and fonts. While these are part of branding, they are not the essence of it. The essence of a brand is how people remember you, and memory is shaped not just by words but by symbols, stories, and experiences.

Jesus understood this. He didn't only preach abstract truths; He embodied them through visible acts, symbolic gestures, and unforgettable stories. He turned water into wine, multiplied bread, washed His disciples' feet, broke bread at the Last

Supper, and used simple objects—coins, lamps, seeds, sheep—to etch eternal lessons into people's minds.

This reveals a powerful principle for us: people may forget what you say, but they will never forget how you made them feel and what they saw you do. In branding, marketing, and sales, your goal is not only to communicate information but also to create experiences and symbols that anchor your message in the memory of your audience.

Why Symbols Matter

Symbols carry meaning beyond words. A cross is more than two intersecting lines—it represents sacrifice, redemption, and love for billions of people. A wedding ring is more than metal—it represents covenant, loyalty, and belonging.

Businesses also rely on symbols:

- Apple's bitten apple is recognized worldwide as a symbol of creativity and innovation.
- McDonald's golden arches immediately signal fast food, convenience, and familiarity.
- Nike's swoosh communicates speed, energy, and action without a single word.

When you create a symbol or visual anchor, you give people something to hold onto emotionally and mentally. The symbol becomes shorthand for your story and values.

Why Stories Stick

Human beings are wired for story. Neuroscience shows that stories activate more parts of the brain than facts alone. A list of data may inform people, but a story transforms them. It gives meaning, emotion, and memory.

Jesus constantly used parables because He knew facts might fade but stories stick. Consider the Prodigal Son (Luke 15). Without using theological jargon, Jesus painted a picture of repentance, grace, jealousy, and restoration through a family story. Two thousand years later, we still tell it because the story is more powerful than a list of principles.

Your brand needs stories the same way. Data and features matter, but stories are what people repeat. Case studies, customer testimonies, and origin stories all become brand parables that carry your message far beyond your marketing.

Why Experiences Transform

Finally, experiences take words and stories and make them tangible. Jesus didn't just talk about humility—He washed His disciples' feet (John 13:3–15). He didn't just speak of covenant—He broke bread and shared wine at the Last Supper (Luke 22:19–20). He didn't just preach abundance—He fed thousands with a few loaves and fish (John 6:1–14).

These actions became signature moves that people never forgot. They weren't random; they were intentional experiences designed to reinforce His message.

In business, experiences matter too. Think about the difference between receiving a generic invoice and receiving a handwritten thank-you note with it. Both accomplish the task of payment, but one creates an experience that deepens loyalty. Or think about walking into a store where the staff knows your name versus one where you're treated like a number. Experiences are the glue of brand memory.

The Danger of Forgettable Brands

The opposite of memorable branding is forgettable branding. This happens when businesses rely only on information. They tell people what they do but don't give them a story, symbol, or experience to remember it by.

For example, imagine a consultant who says, "I help businesses grow revenue." Helpful, but generic. Now imagine a consultant who hands every client a "Growth Roadmap" booklet at the start of their journey and calls it their "Blueprint to Breakthrough." Suddenly, there's a symbol and experience tied to the service. Clients are more likely to remember and share it.

Forgettable brands fade into noise. Memorable brands use symbols, stories, and experiences to carve space in people's minds.

Building Your Own Signature Moves

A signature move is a consistent, repeatable action that embodies your values and makes your brand distinct. It doesn't have to be big or expensive—it just has to be meaningful and consistent. For example:

- A real estate agent could give clients a framed photo of their new home at closing.
- A coach could start every client call with a one-minute affirmation ritual.
- A financial advisor could celebrate milestones with handwritten notes or small gifts.

These touches may seem small, but they create emotional anchors. People remember how you made them feel long after they forget the details of your pitch.

Principle in Summary

Jesus showed us that information alone is not enough. He created a movement that endured by embedding His message in symbols, stories, and signature experiences. As a business leader or entrepreneur, you must do the same. Don't just tell people what you do—show them, give them stories to repeat, and design experiences they'll never forget.

Your brand's power lies not in what you say once, but in what people carry with them after the interaction is over. That's how you build memory, loyalty, and influence that lasts.

Biblical Insight — How Jesus Used Symbols, Stories, and Signature Moves in the Gospels

When we examine the Gospels closely, one thing becomes clear: Jesus did not rely solely on words to communicate His message. He was a master storyteller, a creator of symbols, and a designer of unforgettable experiences. He understood that for truth to endure, it must be embedded not only in the mind but also in the imagination and memory of people. His ministry shows us that spiritual and practical influence flows from what people can see, feel, and remember.

Jesus' Use of Symbols

Throughout the Gospels, Jesus repeatedly employed symbols—physical objects and visible acts that carried spiritual significance. These symbols became anchors for His teachings and left indelible impressions on His audience.

1. Water into Wine (John 2:1–11). At the wedding in Cana, Jesus turned water into wine. This wasn't just a miracle to solve an immediate problem; it was a symbol of transformation, abundance, and joy in the Kingdom of God. The disciples witnessed His glory through a physical sign that pointed to deeper truth.
2. Bread and Wine at the Last Supper (Luke 22:19–20). Perhaps the most enduring symbol Jesus gave us is the breaking of bread and sharing of the cup. These everyday items became reminders of His body broken and His blood shed. To this day, Christians

worldwide repeat this act as communion, keeping His sacrifice central.

3. The Cross. While the cross was originally a Roman instrument of torture and death, Jesus transformed it into a global symbol of salvation, forgiveness, and hope. What was once shameful became the ultimate brand mark of the Gospel.

These examples show how Jesus took ordinary things—wine, bread, wood—and infused them with extraordinary meaning. They became visual anchors that carried His message far beyond His words.

Jesus' Use of Stories

The parables of Jesus are among the most recognized stories in human history. They were not random illustrations but carefully crafted narratives designed to reveal Kingdom truths in relatable ways.

1. The Parable of the Sower (Matthew 13:1–23). Here Jesus used the simple act of planting seeds to illustrate how different hearts respond to God's Word. Everyone in His agrarian culture understood farming, making the story instantly accessible.
2. The Prodigal Son (Luke 15:11–32). This story of rebellion, repentance, and restoration paints a vivid picture of the Father's love. It speaks to emotion,

family, and forgiveness—universal themes that resonate across cultures and centuries.

3. The Good Samaritan (Luke 10:25–37). In answering the question, "Who is my neighbor?" Jesus told a story that challenged prejudice, redefined compassion, and demonstrated love in action.

These parables were memorable because they appealed to imagination and emotion, not just intellect. They could be retold easily, which is why His message spread so effectively through oral tradition. Stories became portable truth—able to travel wherever people went.

Jesus' Use of Signature Moves (Experiential Acts)

Jesus also created signature experiences that embodied His teachings. These weren't just random acts of kindness; they were carefully chosen demonstrations that communicated who He was and what His Kingdom represented.

1. Washing the Disciples' Feet (John 13:3–15). Instead of merely preaching humility, Jesus enacted it. By taking on the role of a servant, He redefined leadership as service. This act was shocking, unforgettable, and impossible to ignore. To this day, the image of Jesus washing feet shapes how we understand servant leadership.

2. Feeding the Five Thousand (John 6:1–14). Jesus could have simply taught about God's provision. Instead, He performed a miracle that everyone experienced firsthand. They ate until satisfied. The act itself became the message: the Kingdom is abundant and generous.
3. Touching the Untouchable (Mark 1:40–42). When Jesus touched and healed a man with leprosy, it wasn't just about physical restoration. It was a bold experiential statement: no one is too unclean for God's love. The action itself dismantled social stigma.
4. Raising Lazarus (John 11:1–44). Jesus didn't only teach about resurrection; He embodied it by calling His friend out of the grave. This signature act of power and compassion confirmed His message in a way words never could.

Each of these experiences acted like a "brand ritual." People remembered them, retold them, and recognized them as uniquely Jesus' way of embodying truth.

Why This Approach Worked

Symbols, stories, and experiences were powerful in Jesus' ministry for several reasons:

- They were relatable. Jesus didn't speak only in lofty theology; He used everyday objects, situations, and human experiences.

- They engaged multiple senses. Hearing a story, seeing a miracle, tasting bread and wine—these involved people fully, not partially.
- They were repeatable. Stories could be retold, communion could be practiced, foot washing could be imitated. His teachings spread because they were transferable.
- They carried emotional weight. Facts inform, but experiences transform. People left not just knowing something new but feeling something unforgettable.

Implications from the Gospels

By consistently using symbols, stories, and signature moves, Jesus created a movement that has lasted over two millennia. Even people who don't identify as Christians know about the Good Samaritan, the Prodigal Son, and the Cross. This shows that truth embedded in symbol and story has greater reach and staying power than truth delivered only as abstract doctrine.

For us, this insight matters because it shows that influence is not just about accuracy—it's about memorability. Jesus' teachings were accurate, but they were also unforgettable because they were embodied.

Conclusion

The Gospels reveal Jesus as a master communicator who used symbols, stories, and signature moves to root His message in the hearts of people. His ministry shows us that influence is not simply about what we say—it's about how we help people experience and remember what we say.

If we want to follow His model in our businesses and leadership, we must learn not only to inform but also to symbolize, to storytell, and to create experiences that reinforce our message. Like Jesus, we must embed truth in memory so that it continues to live long after the words have been spoken.

Business Application — Creating Symbols, Stories, and Signature Moves in Your Brand

The principles of symbols, stories, and signature moves are not just theological insights from the ministry of Jesus; they are also highly practical tools for building a lasting, impactful brand. In today's crowded marketplace, information alone will not set you apart. Everyone has information. What makes people remember, trust, and share your brand are the symbols you create, the stories you tell, and the experiences you design.

Let's explore how you can intentionally apply these lessons in branding, marketing, and sales.

Why Symbols Anchor Your Brand

Symbols are powerful because they condense meaning into a simple, memorable form. In branding, your logo is only the beginning. True brand symbols go deeper—they are images, phrases, and visuals that people immediately associate with you.

- Visual Anchors. Think about Apple's bitten apple or Nike's swoosh. Without words, they communicate identity. But even small businesses can create visual anchors. A realtor might use a key icon in all marketing to symbolize unlocking new beginnings. A financial coach might use a seed logo to symbolize growth and wealth building.
- Ritual Objects. You can also use tangible items as symbolic anchors. A consultant might give every new client a branded journal called "The Breakthrough Book." A gym might give members a wristband that says "Strong Inside Out." These small items carry emotional significance and remind people of your mission.
- Language Symbols. Phrases and taglines can also become symbolic. "Just Do It" is not just a slogan; it's a cultural anchor. For your business, a repeated phrase like "Move from stress to success" or "We turn houses into homes" can become a symbolic shorthand for your entire mission.

Symbols are important because they stick. They are easy to recall and repeat. They allow your brand to live in people's minds without requiring long explanations.

Why Stories Spread Your Message

Every strong brand has a story, and the best brands have multiple stories they can tell repeatedly. Data shows that people remember stories up to 22 times more than facts alone. When you wrap your truth in narrative, people not only understand it—they share it.

Here are three essential stories every brand should develop:

1. The Origin Story. Where did you come from? Why did you start? What problem were you trying to solve? Just as the Gospels tell us the origin of Jesus' ministry, your clients want to know your beginnings. Vulnerability and honesty make this story powerful.
2. The Client Transformation Story. Like Jesus' parables of changed lives, you should have testimonies of clients who went from struggle to success. These become modern parables that prove your promise works in real life.
3. The Future Story. Paint a picture of where your audience could be if they partner with you. This is what Jesus did when He described the Kingdom as a banquet, a harvest, or a treasure. He painted possibilities.

Stories should be repeated across platforms: in sales calls, marketing campaigns, and even casual conversations. If you tell the same core stories consistently, your brand will grow in credibility and recognition.

Why Experiences Build Loyalty

Information informs. Stories inspire. But experiences transform. Customers may forget the details of your product, but they will never forget how you made them feel.

Experiences can be intentional rituals you design to embody your brand's values:

- Onboarding Experiences. Instead of sending a plain invoice after a sale, send a welcome package. Include a handwritten thank-you note, a small symbolic gift, and a clear roadmap of what comes next. This sets the tone.
- Celebration Rituals. Create consistent ways to celebrate client milestones. A real estate agent might give champagne and a photo frame at closing. A coach might host a "graduation" call when clients hit their goals. These experiences cement memories.
- Signature Acts of Service. Think of something small but consistent you can do for every client that makes them feel valued. It might be a personal check-in, a surprise bonus resource, or remembering personal details like birthdays. These touches go beyond transactions and create relationships.

Jesus showed us that experiences are more powerful than words. Washing feet, breaking bread, feeding crowds—these moments were unforgettable. In the same way, businesses that design signature experiences create stories clients can't stop sharing.

Crafting Your Own Signature Move

Every brand should have at least one signature move—a consistent act, phrase, or ritual that becomes associated with you. It doesn't have to be big; it just has to be meaningful and repeatable.

Examples:

- A photographer who gives clients a surprise mini-album after every shoot.
- A restaurant that ends meals with a free small dessert labeled "Our Gift of Gratitude."
- A consultant who sends a personalized video message after every session.

The key is consistency. A signature move becomes a brand marker only when it is repeated enough times for people to expect it and talk about it.

Putting It All Together

To apply this principle, take these practical steps:

1. Define One Symbol. Choose a visual, phrase, or object that represents your brand. Use it consistently.

2. Develop Three Core Stories. Write out your origin story, one transformation story, and one future story. Practice telling them naturally.
3. Design One Signature Experience. Map out how clients will feel when they interact with you. Make at least one moment unforgettable.
4. Create One Signature Move. A small but consistent action that becomes uniquely yours.
5. Repeat Relentlessly. Symbols, stories, and experiences only stick if repeated. Build them into your workflow so they happen automatically.

Conclusion

Jesus demonstrated that words alone are not enough. Symbols give meaning, stories give memorability, and experiences give transformation. When businesses intentionally design these elements into their branding and customer journey, they move beyond transactions to create loyalty and influence.

A forgettable brand tells information. A memorable brand creates symbols, tells stories, and crafts experiences. And the most enduring brands, like Jesus' movement, anchor these practices in values that never change.

Your task is clear: define your symbols, craft your stories, and design your signature moves. Do this consistently, and your brand will not only be remembered—it will be loved, shared, and trusted.

CHAPTER 4

Storytelling Mastery: The Power of Parables

The Principle — Why Storytelling Captures Hearts and Moves People to Action

If there is one communication skill that sets apart those who influence from those who fade into the background, it is storytelling. Numbers can inform, facts can persuade, but stories capture imagination, stir emotion, and compel people to act. In business, leadership, and life, you can deliver all the data in the world, but if people don't feel it, they won't remember it.

Jesus, the greatest communicator in history, mastered storytelling. He rarely taught without using parables. Rather than delivering dry theological lectures, He painted pictures with words. He told stories about farmers sowing seeds, shepherds finding sheep, fathers welcoming prodigal sons, and merchants discovering hidden treasures. These stories didn't just communicate doctrine; they communicated life.

Why Stories Are More Powerful Than Facts

Human beings are wired for story. Neuroscientists have shown that when we hear data, only the language-processing part of our brain engages. But when we hear a story, multiple parts of the brain light up—sensory, emotional, and memory centers. We don't just hear stories; we experience them.

For example, if I tell you, "Our product improves efficiency by 27%," you may nod politely and forget it five minutes later. But if I tell you, "One of our clients was working 70 hours a week, barely seeing his kids. After using our system, he cut that to 45 hours and was able to attend his daughter's soccer games for the first time in months," suddenly you're leaning in. Why? Because the story puts flesh on the facts.

This is why Jesus used parables. He knew that people wouldn't remember abstract theological formulas, but they would remember a father running to embrace a son, a Samaritan stopping to help an injured stranger, or a woman sweeping her house to find a lost coin.

The Simplicity of Storytelling

Another reason storytelling works is that it makes complex truths simple. Theology is complex, business strategy can be overwhelming, and abstract concepts often intimidate. But stories break complexity into pictures. A farmer scattering seeds makes the mystery of faith tangible. A mustard seed growing into a tree explains exponential influence better than any diagram.

In branding and marketing, the same is true. Most businesses drown their audience in jargon: "We provide scalable, data-driven, customer-centric solutions." That's forgettable. But if you say, "We're like a GPS for your business—we help you know exactly where you are and how to get where you want to go," people instantly understand.

Stories Create Emotional Connection

People make decisions emotionally and justify them logically. Stories tap into emotion. They make people feel before they think. That's why Jesus could change hearts with a parable more effectively than a Pharisee could with a lecture.

Consider the Parable of the Prodigal Son. Jesus could have simply said, "God forgives repentant sinners." True, but abstract. Instead, He told a story of a rebellious son, a grieving father, and a joyful homecoming. The listeners didn't just understand forgiveness—they felt it. They saw it. They imagined themselves in it.

Businesses that use storytelling do the same. Instead of saying, "Our service reduces stress," they tell the story of a client who used to lie awake at night worried about finances, but after working with them, now sleeps peacefully. Stories humanize the benefit.

Stories Make Your Brand Portable

One of the most powerful aspects of storytelling is that it makes your message portable. People may not remember your entire pitch or presentation, but they'll remember a story and repeat it to others. That's how word of mouth spreads.

Jesus designed His stories to be easily retold. A Samaritan helps a stranger. A father runs to his son. A shepherd leaves 99 sheep to find one. These were simple, portable, repeatable. That's why they spread from village to village long before they were written down.

Your brand can do the same. If you give people a story about a client's transformation, they can retell it at dinner parties, at networking events, or on social media. You equip your audience to become your marketers.

Stories Create Identity

Stories don't just inform; they form identity. Families are shaped by the stories they tell. Nations are built on shared narratives. Companies create culture through the stories of their founders and milestones.

Jesus' followers were bound together not only by doctrines but by shared stories: "We were there when He fed the 5,000. We saw Him calm the storm. We heard Him say the Kingdom is like a seed." These stories didn't just entertain; they defined who they were as a community.

In the same way, your business needs to cultivate stories that shape your identity. How did you start? What challenges did you overcome? What lives have you changed? These become the stories that unite your team and your customers in a shared sense of mission.

Principle in Practice

If you want to master storytelling in your brand and business, ask yourself:

1. What is my core message? (Jesus' was the Kingdom of God.)
2. What stories illustrate this message? (Parables, client case studies, origin stories.)
3. How can I repeat them in different ways? (Jesus used seeds, coins, sheep—all for the same truth.)
4. How can I make them portable? (Simple, emotional, memorable stories people can retell.)

Your business doesn't need a hundred different stories. It needs a few great ones, told consistently, that embody your brand promise.

Conclusion

The principle of storytelling mastery is simple yet profound: facts tell, stories sell. Jesus demonstrated that truth without story often dies in the ears of the listener, but truth embedded in story lives in their heart.

If you want people to not only hear your message but to carry it, you must become a storyteller. Not a manipulator, not a hype artist, but a genuine communicator who uses stories to illuminate truth, stir emotion, and inspire action.

Just like Jesus' parables still live today, the stories you tell about your work and your clients can live far beyond a single sale—they can become the very identity of your brand.

Biblical Insight — Jesus' Storytelling Through Parables in the Gospels

When we turn to the Gospels, it becomes clear that Jesus was not only a master teacher but also the greatest storyteller who ever lived. His parables were not filler illustrations. They were His primary teaching method, chosen with divine intentionality to reveal the mysteries of the Kingdom of God in a way that would resonate deeply with the hearts and minds of ordinary people.

The word parable comes from the Greek word parabole, which means "to place alongside." A parable is a story placed alongside a truth to help explain it. Rather than simply delivering abstract theology, Jesus placed truth next to everyday life experiences—farming, fishing, family conflict, money, celebrations—so that people could see themselves in the story and grasp the message.

The Centrality of Parables in Jesus' Teaching

Matthew records that Jesus "spoke all these things to the crowd in parables; he did not say anything to them without using a parable" (Matthew 13:34). That's a bold statement. It shows that parables were not occasional teaching aids—they were His central method.

Why? Because Jesus wasn't trying to impress the educated elite with intellectual arguments. He wanted to reach the common person, the farmer, the fisherman, the homemaker, the tax collector. By using parables, He made eternal truths accessible without diluting their power.

Parables also had a dual purpose: they revealed truth to those who were hungry for it and concealed truth from those who were hardened against it (Matthew 13:10–17). For the spiritually curious, a parable opened a door. For the cynical or arrogant, it left them puzzled. This tension forced listeners to lean in, to ask questions, to wrestle with meaning.

Key Themes in Jesus' Parables

Although Jesus told dozens of parables, they consistently pointed to key themes of the Kingdom:

1. Growth and Multiplication.
    - Parable of the Sower (Matthew 13:1–23): Different soils represented different responses

to the Word. Growth depended not on the seed but on the condition of the heart.

- Parable of the Mustard Seed (Matthew 13:31–32): The Kingdom starts small but grows into something massive, impacting nations.

2. Value and Treasure.
   - Parable of the Hidden Treasure and the Pearl of Great Price (Matthew 13:44–46): The Kingdom is so valuable that it's worth giving up everything to obtain it.

3. Compassion and Forgiveness.
   - Parable of the Prodigal Son (Luke 15:11–32): The Father's heart for restoration is unmatched.
   - Parable of the Unforgiving Servant (Matthew 18:21–35): Forgiveness received must become forgiveness extended.

4. Readiness and Stewardship.
   - Parable of the Ten Virgins (Matthew 25:1–13): Be prepared for the coming of the Bridegroom.
   - Parable of the Talents (Matthew 25:14–30): Steward resources faithfully because accountability is coming.

5. Love and Neighborliness.
   - Parable of the Good Samaritan (Luke 10:25–37): Love crosses social and cultural boundaries.

Through these stories, Jesus revealed the values, priorities, and nature of the Kingdom. He wasn't just telling stories to entertain; He was shaping worldview, challenging assumptions, and inviting transformation.

The Impact of Parables on Audiences

Parables cut through social and cultural barriers. For example, in the Parable of the Good Samaritan, Jesus deliberately chose a Samaritan—a despised outsider—as the hero of the story. To His Jewish audience, this was shocking, even offensive. Yet it forced them to confront their prejudices and rethink what it meant to love one's neighbor.

In the Parable of the Prodigal Son, listeners could identify with each character: the rebellious son, the forgiving father, or the bitter older brother. By seeing themselves in the story, they couldn't dismiss the lesson—it hit too close to home.

Parables also endured because they were memorable. People may forget abstract teaching points, but they remember images: a seed, a lamp, a sheep, a coin. These images stuck in minds and hearts, ready to resurface when life situations mirrored the story.

Parables as a Marketing Blueprint

Interestingly, the way Jesus used parables mirrors what great communicators and marketers do today. They take a truth and wrap it in story so that people feel it and remember it. Parables made Jesus' message portable. A farmer who heard the Parable of the Sower could go home and tell it to his family. A housewife who heard about the lost coin could repeat it to her neighbors. These weren't complex theological lectures—they were viral stories.

This explains why Jesus' influence spread so quickly. His stories weren't just deep; they were shareable. In today's language, they were "sticky content."

Lessons We Learn from Jesus' Storytelling

1. Use the Familiar to Teach the Eternal. Jesus used everyday images people already understood. Don't overcomplicate your message—tie it to what people already know.
2. Engage Emotion, Not Just Intellect. Parables made people feel—whether joy, conviction, or surprise. Aim for the heart, not just the head.
3. Leave Room for Reflection. Parables often ended without full explanation, forcing listeners to wrestle. In the same way, stories that invite people to think last longer than lectures.
4. Be Consistent with Themes. Jesus' parables were diverse, but all pointed to the Kingdom. Your stories should be diverse in expression but consistent in message.

Conclusion

The Gospels present Jesus as a master of parables, weaving truth into story so deeply that it still resonates centuries later. His stories reveal the nature of the Kingdom, challenge assumptions, and invite transformation.

For us, the biblical insight is clear: if we want our message—whether spiritual, personal, or business-related—to stick, we must learn from Jesus. Information without story is forgettable. Information embedded in story becomes unforgettable.

This is why Jesus' parables still echo through history. They were not just tales; they were truths wrapped in narrative. And for us, they remain a divine blueprint for how to communicate in ways that move people to think, feel, and act.

Business Application — Using Storytelling in Branding, Marketing, and Sales

Storytelling is not just a communication tool; it is the backbone of branding, marketing, and sales. Products can be copied. Prices can be matched. Features can be improved upon. But the story behind your brand—the narrative that captures hearts and makes your audience feel part of something bigger—is uniquely yours.

Jesus demonstrated this truth perfectly. He didn't simply list theological doctrines; He told parables that wrapped truth in stories. These stories were portable, emotional, and unforgettable. In the same way, if you want your brand to stick in the minds and hearts of your audience, you must learn to tell stories that communicate your mission and value.

Why Stories Sell

At its core, every purchase is a story. People don't buy products—they buy better versions of themselves. They buy into a story of transformation. A woman doesn't just buy a dress; she buys the story of confidence she'll feel wearing it. A man doesn't just buy financial coaching; he buys the story of sleeping peacefully at night instead of worrying about bills.

When your marketing and sales lean on facts alone—"our system is 25% faster," "our homes have 300 more square feet," "our service costs less"—you're competing on commodities. But when you frame your product as part of a story—"this tool will help you spend more evenings with your kids," "this house will be the place your grandkids will visit for years to come"—you elevate your brand into transformation.

The Elements of Effective Storytelling in Business

1. The Hero. In business storytelling, the hero is not you—it's your customer. They are the main character in search of transformation.
2. The Villain. Every story needs conflict. In business, the villain might be stress, confusion, wasted money,

wasted time, or even fear. The clearer you make the villain, the more powerful your story.

3. The Guide. That's you. Just like Jesus acted as the wise teacher guiding listeners through stories, your role is to guide your customer to victory. You're not the hero; you're the mentor who helps the hero succeed.
4. The Transformation. This is the heart of the story. What does life look like before and after working with you? This transformation is your brand promise.

For example, instead of saying, "We sell affordable insurance," tell the story: "A client of ours used to live with constant anxiety about accidents. After joining us, he now lives with peace of mind knowing his family is protected."

How to Use Storytelling in Branding

Branding is the story you consistently tell about who you are, what you value, and how you serve. If your brand lacks story, it feels hollow. Here's how to integrate storytelling into branding:

- Tell Your Origin Story. Why did you start this business? What problem moved you so much that you had to create a solution? People don't just buy what you sell—they buy why you sell it.
- Share Transformation Stories. Use client testimonials not just as reviews but as narratives. Highlight where they started, the challenge they faced, and how your brand helped them overcome it.

- Use Symbolic Stories. Tie your brand values to stories. For example, if one of your values is perseverance, tell the story of your first big obstacle and how you overcame it.

How to Use Storytelling in Marketing

Marketing is where stories spread. Campaigns that work are not lists of features but stories that resonate. Think of Super Bowl commercials—people don't remember the specs of the product; they remember the story.

- Create Campaign Narratives. Instead of running random ads, build campaigns around a central story. For example, a realtor might run a series of ads showing different families finding their "dream home"—a single mom, a young couple, a retired couple—each one a short story tied to the bigger message: "Your next chapter starts here."
- Leverage Video. Storytelling is most powerful when people can see and hear it. Video content allows you to showcase transformation visually and emotionally.
- Use Stories on Social Media. Rather than only posting promotions, share behind-the-scenes stories, client wins, and even small daily moments that reveal your brand's heart.

How to Use Storytelling in Sales

Sales conversations can often feel transactional, but when you weave in stories, they become relational. Stories lower defenses, spark curiosity, and build trust.

- Tell a Client Story. Instead of saying, "Our process works," tell the story of a client who struggled with the same issue your prospect has and how they found success through you.
- Use Micro-Stories. Sales doesn't always require long parables. A quick anecdote—"I had a client just like you who..."—can shift the entire conversation.
- Paint the Future Story. Show the prospect what their life will look like if they say yes. Let them imagine themselves as the hero of the story you're offering.

The Dangers of Storyless Business

If you don't use storytelling, you risk becoming a commodity. People will compare you only by price or features. You'll struggle to stand out in a crowded market. Worse, your brand will be forgettable. Facts fade, but stories live.

Think of Jesus' opponents—the Pharisees. They offered endless rules, lectures, and debates. Yet history doesn't remember their speeches. It remembers Jesus' parables. The same applies to your business. If you rely on information alone, you'll fade. If you weave your truth into stories, you'll endure.

Practical Steps

1. Write Your Core Stories. Develop three: your origin story, one powerful client transformation, and one future story.
2. Practice Storytelling in Conversations. Use them naturally in pitches, networking, and everyday conversations.
3. Collect Stories. Actively ask clients for testimonies and frame them as stories, not just reviews.
4. Repeat Consistently. Just like Jesus reused Kingdom parables in different ways, retell your stories across different platforms.

Conclusion

Storytelling is not a "nice extra"—it's the heart of influence. In branding, it creates identity. In marketing, it creates resonance. In sales, it creates trust. Jesus modeled this with His parables, embedding eternal truths in unforgettable narratives.

For you, the call is clear: don't just describe what you do—tell the story of why it matters and how it transforms lives. When you master storytelling, your brand will not just be seen or heard—it will be remembered, repeated, and cherished.

CHAPTER 5

Word of Mouth: Go and Tell

The Principle — Why Word of Mouth Is the Most Powerful Marketing

If you stripped away all the advertising platforms, removed every billboard, silenced every television commercial, and deleted every social media account, how would businesses grow? The answer is simple: word of mouth. Long before there were algorithms, ad campaigns, and media budgets, word of mouth was the original and most effective marketing strategy. And even today, in a world of endless digital noise, word of mouth remains the most trusted form of influence.

Jesus modeled this principle perfectly. He didn't have a website, a marketing team, or a budget. Yet His message spread across villages, cities, nations, and eventually the world. How? People encountered Him, experienced transformation, and couldn't help but tell others. The Samaritan woman at the well ran back to her town saying, "Come, see a man who told me everything I ever did" (John 4:29). The formerly demon-possessed man in the Decapolis went out proclaiming what Jesus had done for him (Mark 5:20). The blind, the lame, the healed, and the forgiven became walking billboards for the Kingdom.

That's the essence of word of mouth: people who have been impacted share their experience with others.

Why Word of Mouth Works

Word of mouth is powerful because it is rooted in trust. People may not trust an ad, but they trust their friend, coworker, or family member. When someone you know says, "This changed my life" or "You've got to try this," it carries weight.

Research confirms this: studies show that over 90% of consumers trust recommendations from people they know more than any form of advertising. In fact, word of mouth is estimated to influence between 20–50% of all purchasing decisions. It's not just marketing—it's the most persuasive marketing.

Why? Because word of mouth is relational, not transactional. Ads are designed to sell; friends are motivated to help. When someone shares their story with you, it feels personal and credible.

The Nature of Organic Spread

Word of mouth often starts small but grows organically. One person tells another. That person tells two more. Soon, the message spreads far beyond the original circle. Think about how news spreads in a community: one person sees something remarkable, shares it with neighbors, and suddenly everyone knows.

This is exactly how Jesus' influence spread. In Luke 7:16–17, after He raised a widow's son, the text says: "They were all filled with awe and praised God. A great prophet has appeared among us… This news about Jesus spread throughout Judea and the surrounding country." He performed one act of compassion, and the story traveled on the lips of those who witnessed it.

Word of mouth thrives on stories. People don't just share information—they share narratives. "I saw it with my own eyes," "I was there," "This happened to me." That's why it spreads so quickly.

The Viral Nature of Testimony

Word of mouth is essentially testimony. It is one person giving witness to what they've seen, heard, or experienced. Jesus leaned heavily on this principle. In Acts 1:8, before ascending to heaven, He told His disciples: "You will be my witnesses." Not just preachers, not just debaters, but witnesses. Witnesses tell their story of what they've experienced.

Testimony is viral because it's personal. It's not theory—it's lived truth. When someone says, "I was blind but now I see," there's no argument against it. When someone says, "I was drowning in debt and this plan helped me become debt-free," it resonates because it's real.

That's the secret of word of mouth: it's not about perfect packaging, it's about authentic experience.

The Risk of Silence

The opposite of word of mouth is silence. A satisfied customer who says nothing helps no one. A transformed life that doesn't share the story misses the opportunity to multiply impact.

Jesus constantly encouraged people to share what they had experienced. To the healed demoniac in Mark 5:19 He said, "Go home to your own people and tell them how much the Lord has done for you, and how he has had mercy on you." Transformation was never meant to be hidden—it was meant to be told.

For businesses, the same is true. If you don't intentionally encourage your customers to share their stories, you are leaving the most powerful marketing channel untapped.

Word of Mouth vs. Paid Marketing

Does this mean you should never use paid advertising? Not at all. Paid marketing has its place. But word of mouth is the foundation. Paid ads can amplify awareness, but they cannot replace the trust that comes from personal recommendation.

Think of it this way: a paid ad is a stranger talking to you; word of mouth is a friend talking to you. Which will you trust more? Exactly.

This is why the most effective paid campaigns often include real customer stories, reviews, or testimonials. They borrow credibility from word of mouth because they know that's what moves people.

Principle in Summary

The principle is simple yet profound: word of mouth is the most effective, enduring, and persuasive form of marketing. It builds trust because it's relational. It spreads naturally because it's rooted in story. It multiplies influence because it's personal and real.

Jesus built a movement on word of mouth, not media buys. His followers became witnesses, and their stories became the engine of the Gospel's spread. In the same way, your brand will grow when your customers, clients, and community become your storytellers.

If you want sustainable influence, don't just focus on what you say—focus on creating experiences that people will want to talk about. That's the true engine of word of mouth.

Biblical Insight — Word of Mouth in the Gospels and Acts

When we trace the growth of Jesus' influence in the Gospels and the early church in Acts, one truth emerges: the Kingdom of God spread primarily through witness and word of mouth. Jesus did not publish books, rent advertising space, or establish a broadcasting network. Instead, ordinary people who had extraordinary encounters with Him became the carriers of His message. Their testimonies traveled farther than any campaign could, igniting movements that continue to this day.

Word of Mouth in the Ministry of Jesus

The Samaritan Woman (John 4:1–42)

One of the clearest examples of word of mouth is the Samaritan woman at the well. After her encounter with Jesus, she ran back to her village proclaiming: "Come, see a man who told me everything I ever did. Could this be the Messiah?" (John 4:29). Scripture tells us, "Many of the Samaritans from that town believed in him because of the woman's testimony" (John 4:39).

Notice the sequence: Jesus impacted one person. That person immediately shared her story. Others came not because Jesus directly reached them but because her words stirred curiosity. Then, after meeting Him, they said, "We no longer believe just because of what you said; now we have heard for ourselves" (John 4:42). This is the perfect illustration of how word of mouth works: personal testimony draws people in, and direct experience seals their belief.

The Man Freed from Demons (Mark 5:1–20)

In another striking account, Jesus healed a man possessed by many demons in the region of the Decapolis. After his deliverance, the man begged to follow Jesus. But Jesus told him instead: "Go home to your own people and tell them how much the Lord has done for you, and how he has had mercy on you" (Mark 5:19). The text says, "So the man went away and began to tell in the Decapolis how much Jesus had done for him. And all the people were amazed" (Mark 5:20).

Here, Jesus intentionally deployed word of mouth. Instead of bringing the man along as a disciple, He sent him back into his community as a witness. This single story of transformation became the spark for amazement across an entire region.

News Spreading After Miracles

Over and over again, the Gospels note that news about Jesus "spread." After He healed Jairus's daughter, Matthew records: "News of this spread through all that region" (Matthew 9:26). After healing two blind men, "the news spread about him all over that region" (Matthew 9:31). After cleansing a leper, "news about him spread all the more, so that crowds of people came to hear him and to be healed" (Luke 5:15).

These verses emphasize that it wasn't just Jesus proclaiming Himself—it was others sharing what they had seen, heard, and experienced. Word of mouth was the megaphone of His ministry.

Word of Mouth in the Early Church

The book of Acts shows how this principle carried forward after Jesus' resurrection.

The Apostles as Witnesses

In Acts 1:8, Jesus gave His disciples their final commission: "You will be my witnesses in Jerusalem, and in all Judea and Samaria, and to the ends of the earth." Notice that He didn't say, "You will be my marketers" or "You will be my philosophers." He said "witnesses." A witness simply tells what they have seen and heard.

At Pentecost (Acts 2), when the Holy Spirit was poured out, the disciples began boldly proclaiming what they had witnessed. Three thousand people were added that day—not because of a strategic marketing plan, but because of Spirit-empowered testimony.

Everyday Believers Sharing the Message

Acts also records that persecution scattered the believers from Jerusalem. Instead of silencing the movement, it spread it. Acts

8:4 says, "Those who had been scattered preached the word wherever they went." These weren't professional preachers—just ordinary people sharing extraordinary news.

By Acts 17:6, opponents were saying of the Christians: "These men who have turned the world upside down have come here also." How did a small group of Galilean disciples "turn the world upside down"? Through relentless testimony. Word of mouth carried the Gospel across cities and continents.

Characteristics of Biblical Word of Mouth

From these accounts, we see several key characteristics of biblical word of mouth:

1. Personal. Testimony flowed out of personal experience. "This is what He did for me." That made it credible and compelling.
2. Immediate. People didn't wait until they were polished speakers; they shared as soon as they experienced transformation.
3. Relational. Testimonies spread along natural lines of relationship—family, neighbors, villages, marketplaces.
4. Viral. One story triggered curiosity, which led to encounters, which produced more stories. It multiplied quickly.
5. Empowered. The Spirit amplified word of mouth, turning simple testimonies into movements.

Why Jesus Chose Word of Mouth

Jesus' reliance on word of mouth wasn't accidental. It was strategic. By choosing this method, He ensured that the message was not dependent on one man's voice but could spread through countless voices. It decentralized influence and made it unstoppable.

If His movement had depended only on His personal preaching, it would have ended with His death. Instead, because it was fueled by witnesses, it multiplied after His ascension. The more people tried to silence it, the more it spread.

Lessons for Us

The biblical pattern of word of mouth teaches us:

- The most effective influence is relational. Ads may raise awareness, but transformation shared by a friend changes lives.
- You don't need perfection—just authenticity. The Samaritan woman didn't have theology figured out, but her testimony moved a town.
- Multiplication beats addition. One transformed life telling ten others multiplies impact faster than one person trying to reach everyone alone.

Conclusion

The Gospels and Acts reveal that Jesus and His followers relied on word of mouth as their primary growth engine. Transformed people became storytellers, and their stories spread the Kingdom faster than any organized campaign could.

For us, this is not just history—it's instruction. If we want to influence, grow movements, or build brands that last, we must harness the same principle. Word of mouth is not just an ancient tool; it is God's chosen strategy for spreading truth.

Business Application — Turning Customers into Witnesses for Your Brand

If Jesus built His ministry on the strength of people telling others what they had seen, experienced, and believed, then modern businesses and leaders should pay attention. Word of mouth is not just a biblical principle—it's also the most effective marketing channel in today's marketplace. Paid advertising can get you exposure, but word of mouth gets you trust. And in an age where people are bombarded with ads every day, trust is the ultimate currency.

Why Word of Mouth Is Still King

Despite all the innovations in digital marketing—SEO, social ads, influencer partnerships, email funnels—word of mouth remains the most persuasive force in buying decisions. Research consistently shows that recommendations from friends, family, and peers are more trusted than any other form of advertising. People may scroll past an ad, but when a coworker says, "This company changed my life," they lean in.

Think about your own decisions. The last time you tried a new restaurant, bought a new gadget, or hired a service, what influenced you most? Probably not an ad—it was a friend's recommendation, an online review, or a personal story. That's word of mouth in action.

Businesses that fail to harness this principle end up spending more on advertising to make up for the credibility they lack. Businesses that embrace it grow faster and more sustainably, because satisfied customers do the marketing for them.

The Nature of Modern Testimony

In the Gospels, testimony spread through villages and marketplaces. Today, it spreads both face-to-face and online. Modern word of mouth includes:

- Reviews and Ratings. Sites like Google, Yelp, and Amazon amplify customer voices. A 5-star review is today's equivalent of someone telling their neighbor, "This really works."
- Social Media Sharing. Customers post experiences, tag businesses, and share transformations with their networks.

- Testimonials and Case Studies. Written, video, or live testimonies from clients provide modern parables of transformation.
- Influencer Endorsements. Though often paid, the effectiveness of influencer marketing still comes down to word of mouth—a trusted voice recommending a product.

The principle hasn't changed—just the platforms. Testimonies still carry the most weight, because they're personal, relatable, and real.

How to Turn Customers into Witnesses

1. Deliver an Experience Worth Talking About.
   Word of mouth starts with impact. People only share stories when something exceeds expectations. If your service is average, you won't be talked about. If your product solves a problem in a way that feels life-changing, people can't help but share. Focus first on creating remarkable experiences.

2. Ask for the Story, Not Just the Sale.
   Many businesses forget to invite customers to share their experiences. After you've delivered value, ask: "Would you be willing to share your story?" Frame it as storytelling, not just a review. This creates richer, more emotional testimonies.

3. Make Sharing Easy.
   Give customers tools to spread the word. Provide shareable graphics, hashtags, or referral codes. Make leaving reviews simple with direct links. The easier it is to share, the more likely they will.

4. Highlight Customer Stories Publicly.
   Just as Jesus highlighted the faith of the woman with the issue of blood (Luke 8:48), you can celebrate customer wins publicly. Post their stories on your website, feature them in newsletters, or showcase them on social media. When people see others celebrated, they're more likely to share too.

5. Create a Referral System.
   Encourage word of mouth intentionally by rewarding it. Offer discounts, bonuses, or gifts for referrals. But keep it authentic—customers should feel like they're recommending you because they believe in you, not just because of the reward.

The Power of Story-Driven Marketing

Every time a client tells their story, your brand gains credibility. But don't just collect reviews—shape them into stories. For example:

- Instead of: "The service was great." Say: "Before working with this company, I was drowning in

> paperwork. Now I finish in half the time and actually enjoy my evenings again."

That's transformation. That's testimony. That's a story others can see themselves in.

The best brands curate dozens of these stories and share them across platforms. Over time, these stories become modern parables—just like the healed, the forgiven, and the restored spread the fame of Jesus.

Turning Employees Into Witnesses

Word of mouth doesn't just come from customers—it comes from your team. Employees who believe in the mission become some of the most powerful witnesses. When they talk passionately about their workplace to friends and family, they spread brand credibility far beyond official channels.

That's why culture matters. Treat your team well, invest in them, and they'll naturally become advocates. Just like the disciples shared what they saw and experienced with Jesus, your employees will share what they experience with you.

Pitfalls to Avoid

1. Forcing the Story. If testimonies feel scripted or fake, they lose credibility. Authenticity is non-negotiable.

2. Ignoring Negative Word of Mouth. People will talk whether you want them to or not. Address complaints quickly and transparently—turn critics into fans by how you handle issues.
3. Being Inconsistent. If your service doesn't match your promise, word of mouth can hurt you instead of help you. Remember, people share bad experiences faster than good ones.

Practical Action Steps

- Identify 3–5 clients whose stories showcase your brand promise. Ask permission to feature their testimonies.
- Build a referral program that rewards sharing but keeps authenticity intact.
- Incorporate story prompts into follow-up emails: "What was life like before working with us? What's different now?"
- Dedicate one content channel (blog, newsletter, video series) to telling customer stories.
- Train your team to ask for stories naturally during conversations.

Conclusion

Turning customers into witnesses is not a marketing trick—it's the biblical principle of testimony applied to business. Just as the Samaritan woman, the healed demoniac, and the apostles spread the Gospel through their stories, your customers can spread your brand through theirs.

When you deliver experiences worth talking about, invite people to share, and amplify their stories, you unleash the most powerful form of marketing: word of mouth. It's relational, trustworthy, and enduring. Ads may win attention, but testimonies win hearts.

If Jesus built a global movement on word of mouth, imagine what your business can do when your customers become your storytellers.

CHAPTER 6

Building a Core Team: The Twelve

The Principle — Why Every Vision Needs a Core Team

No matter how gifted, skilled, or visionary a leader may be, no movement grows or endures without a team. Lone rangers burn out. Solo leaders plateau. Visionaries without structure fizzle out. But leaders who intentionally build a core team create impact that multiplies beyond themselves.

Jesus, though fully divine, demonstrated this principle in His earthly ministry. He could have done everything alone—preaching, healing, traveling. But instead, He chose to invest deeply in a small group of disciples who would become the foundation of the church. By building a team of twelve, Jesus showed us that success in any mission—whether ministry, business, or leadership—depends not on the strength of one but on the commitment of many.

Why You Need a Core Team

Every great business or movement requires a core group of people who:

- Believe in the mission.
- Carry the culture.
- Multiply the message.
- Extend the influence.

Without a core team, leaders are stretched thin. They may generate activity, but not sustainability. A leader without a team is like a firework—bright, exciting, but short-lived. A leader with a core team is like a campfire—steady, enduring, and able to ignite others.

Core Teams Create Multiplication

The power of a team is not just in what they can do together but in how they can multiply influence. If one person works alone, their impact is limited to their personal capacity. But if one person invests in twelve, and those twelve each reach others, the impact grows exponentially. This is the principle of multiplication versus addition.

Many entrepreneurs and leaders fall into the trap of addition: they work harder, add more hours, take on more responsibilities, and stretch themselves thin. But Jesus demonstrated multiplication: invest deeply in a few, and those few will carry the mission forward.

Core Teams Carry Culture

Culture is not taught—it's caught. A leader can write down values on paper, but if no one embodies them, they remain abstract. A core team ensures that the DNA of the mission is replicated.

Think of a restaurant. The owner can't serve every table. But if the core staff—managers, chefs, servers—carry the culture of excellence and hospitality, every customer feels the same experience. In business, your core team becomes the living expression of your values.

Core Teams Provide Support

Leadership is demanding. Without support, leaders burn out. A core team provides encouragement, accountability, and shared responsibility. Jesus had moments of weariness and even grief (like in Gethsemane), and He leaned on His inner circle. Leaders today need the same. No one can carry vision alone.

Core Teams Outlast Leaders

The greatest proof of a leader's effectiveness is what happens after they're gone. If everything collapses when the leader steps away, the foundation was weak. But if the mission continues, the leader has succeeded. Jesus' core team carried His message after His ascension, proving that a strong core team ensures legacy.

In business, if your company only thrives when you're present, you haven't built a core team—you've built dependency. True leadership builds independence in others so the mission can outlast the founder.

Choosing Depth Over Width

One of the most important principles Jesus demonstrated was depth over width. He ministered to crowds but invested in twelve. Within the twelve, He invested even more deeply in three (Peter, James, John). This shows us that while broad influence is good, deep investment in a few creates the strongest impact.

Many leaders spread themselves too thin, trying to mentor everyone. The wiser approach is to go deep with a few and let them multiply the culture. In business, this means choosing a handful of key people—partners, managers, or team leads—to invest in consistently.

Principle in Practice

If you want to follow Jesus' model of building a core team:

1. Identify the Mission. Be clear on what you're building. A core team cannot exist around confusion.

2. Choose the Right People. Look for commitment, teachability, and alignment with your values—not just talent.
3. Invest in Them Deeply. Spend time mentoring, equipping, and empowering them.
4. Model the Culture. Let them see you live the values you want them to carry.
5. Release Responsibility. Don't just keep them close—send them out to extend the mission.

Conclusion

The principle is undeniable: every lasting movement is built on a core team. Jesus modeled it with the Twelve, and leaders in every field must embrace it. Whether you're growing a business, leading a ministry, or launching a new project, the size of your crowd matters less than the strength of your core.

Invest in a few, and they will carry the mission to many. Build a strong core team, and your vision will not only grow—it will endure.

Biblical Insight — Jesus and the Twelve in the Gospels

When we study the Gospels, one of the most striking aspects of Jesus' ministry is His deliberate choice to build a team of twelve disciples. He did not merely gather a crowd, nor did He depend solely on His own divine authority to carry the mission forward. Instead, He invested deeply in a small group of ordinary men and, through them, laid the foundation of a global movement. This decision was intentional, strategic, and full of lessons for anyone seeking to build something lasting.

The Calling of the Twelve

The Synoptic Gospels all record the moment Jesus formally called the Twelve. Luke's account is especially detailed:

"One of those days Jesus went out to a mountainside to pray, and spent the night praying to God. When morning came, he called his disciples to him and chose twelve of them, whom he also designated apostles" (Luke 6:12–13).

This moment highlights two key truths:

1. Prayerful Selection. Jesus didn't rush into choosing His team. He spent an entire night in prayer, seeking the Father's wisdom. His choice was guided by divine insight, not human guesswork.
2. Intentional Designation. He didn't just invite them to follow; He appointed them as apostles—messengers who would be sent. From the very beginning, the plan was not just for them to learn but to eventually carry the mission forward.

This teaches us that choosing a core team requires both prayerful discernment and intentionality. The right people are not always the most obvious or impressive but those who are aligned with the mission and willing to grow.

The Diversity of the Twelve

The Twelve were not chosen for their similarity but for their diversity. Among them were:

- Fishermen (Peter, Andrew, James, John).
- A tax collector (Matthew).
- A zealot (Simon the Zealot, part of a revolutionary group).
- A skeptic (Thomas).
- A betrayer (Judas Iscariot).

Jesus didn't pick twelve of the same personality or background. Instead, He brought together a diverse group who would each contribute unique perspectives and skills. This diversity ensured that the movement could reach a wide range of people.

For us, this shows that a strong core team is not about cloning ourselves but about building a body with different strengths that complement one another.

The Inner Circle

Within the Twelve, Jesus had an inner circle: Peter, James, and John. These three were present at key moments like the raising of Jairus's daughter (Mark 5:37), the Transfiguration (Mark 9:2), and the prayer in Gethsemane (Mark 14:33).

Why did Jesus focus more deeply on three? Because depth of investment multiplies strength. By pouring more intentionally into a smaller group within the larger team, He ensured that even when others faltered, the mission would still have strong anchors. Peter later became the bold leader at Pentecost, John became the apostle of love and author of five New Testament books, and James became the first apostolic martyr. The inner circle carried extraordinary weight because of their closeness to Jesus.

Training Through Experience

Jesus didn't just lecture the Twelve. He trained them through hands-on experience. He sent them out two by two (Mark 6:7–13) to preach, heal, and cast out demons. They returned with reports, and He debriefed them, correcting and encouraging.

This on-the-job training was crucial. They weren't just hearing His teaching; they were practicing it. They failed at times (like when they couldn't cast out a demon in Mark 9:17–18), but even failure became part of their growth. Jesus patiently corrected them, teaching them that success wasn't about technique but about faith and dependence on God.

Modeling Leadership

The disciples didn't just hear what Jesus taught; they watched how He lived. They saw Him pray alone at night, show compassion to crowds, challenge the Pharisees, heal the sick, and serve the poor. They were close enough to witness His tears, His frustrations, and His moments of deep compassion.

Jesus didn't hide His humanity. By modeling authentic leadership, He gave the disciples an example they could imitate. As He later told them: "I have set you an example that you should do as I have done for you" (John 13:15).

Sending Them Out

Near the end of His ministry, Jesus began to release more responsibility to His disciples. In Matthew 28:19–20, He commissioned them: "Go and make disciples of all nations, baptizing them in the name of the Father and of the Son and of the Holy Spirit, and teaching them to obey everything I have commanded you."

This moment shows that His investment in the Twelve was never meant to terminate in them. They were trained to multiply. His vision was not just twelve men growing in faith but twelve men carrying His mission to the world.

The Weaknesses of the Twelve

Interestingly, the Gospels are honest about the flaws of the Twelve. Peter denied Jesus three times. Thomas doubted. James and John argued about greatness. Judas betrayed Him. This shows us that Jesus didn't choose perfect people—He chose willing people.

The weakness of the Twelve is actually part of the lesson. Teams don't have to be flawless to be effective. What matters most is their connection to the leader and their commitment to the mission. Jesus' grace covered their failures and His Spirit empowered their transformation.

Lessons From Jesus' Team

From the Gospels, we learn these essential truths about building a core team:

1. Pray Before Choosing. Don't select based only on skill—seek divine wisdom.
2. Diversity Adds Strength. Different backgrounds and personalities enrich the team.
3. Go Deep With a Few. An inner circle creates anchors of strength.
4. Train Through Experience. Give opportunities, allow mistakes, and debrief.
5. Model the Mission. Let them see your life, not just hear your words.

6. Send Them Out. Don't cling to your team—empower them to lead and multiply.

Conclusion

The Gospels reveal that Jesus' greatest earthly strategy wasn't preaching to crowds—it was pouring into a core team. By calling, training, modeling for, and commissioning the Twelve, He ensured that His mission would continue after His earthly ministry ended.

For us, the lesson is unmistakable: leadership is not about doing everything ourselves but about equipping others to carry the mission. A vision becomes a movement only when it is entrusted to a core team who will embody it, expand it, and endure beyond the founder.

Business Application — Building and Leading Your Core Team in Business

If Jesus, the Son of God, chose not to carry His mission alone but instead built and invested in a core team, then leaders today—whether in ministry, business, or entrepreneurship—should recognize the same truth: no vision can grow, scale, or endure without a strong inner circle. In business terms, your "Twelve" might not be fishermen or tax collectors, but they are the people who will carry your culture, multiply your mission, and ensure your brand survives beyond you.

Why Businesses Rise and Fall on Teams

You can have the best product, the most innovative idea, or the clearest vision, but if you don't have the right team, your growth will stall. In fact, many businesses fail not because the idea was weak but because the team was misaligned. Teams determine culture, and culture determines longevity.

Consider startups. Investors often say they invest in teams, not just products. Why? Because a strong team can pivot, adapt, and overcome challenges, while a weak team collapses under pressure. Jesus built a team not because He needed help in a divine sense but because He was modeling the pathway to sustainable impact: invest in a few, and they will multiply the mission far beyond your personal capacity.

Identifying Your "Twelve"

How do you know who belongs in your core team? Not everyone qualifies. Crowds may follow you, but only a few should be close enough to carry your culture. Here are qualities to look for:

1. Alignment With Vision. Skills can be taught, but shared vision cannot. If someone doesn't believe in your mission, they won't carry it forward.
2. Character. Integrity, humility, and resilience matter more than raw talent. Judas was talented with money but lacked character—and it destroyed him.

3. Teachability. Jesus chose ordinary men, not experts, because they were teachable. A teachable spirit outweighs years of experience.
4. Commitment. Your core team must be willing to sacrifice comfort for mission. They're not just employees—they're partners in purpose.
5. Diversity. Just as Jesus chose fishermen, a tax collector, a zealot, and others, diversity strengthens perspective and reach.

Selecting your "Twelve" is about discernment. It's better to go slow and choose right than rush and regret later.

Training Your Team

Building a team doesn't stop at selection—it requires investment. Jesus didn't just call the Twelve; He lived with them, taught them, corrected them, and empowered them. In business, this means creating rhythms of training, mentoring, and shared experience.

Practical ways to train your team:

- Model the Culture. Live the values you want them to embody. If you want a culture of excellence, show excellence in your own work.
- Teach Consistently. Don't just assign tasks; explain the "why" behind decisions. Repetition builds culture.

- Give Real Responsibility. Let your team handle projects that stretch them. Failure will teach as much as success.
- Debrief Often. Create space to reflect on wins and losses. Jesus often pulled His disciples aside after ministry moments to explain or clarify (Mark 4:34).

Training is not just about skill—it's about imparting identity and mission.

Creating an Inner Circle

Within your core team, you'll have an "inner three" like Jesus had with Peter, James, and John. These are the people who have the closest access to you, who see you in moments of strength and vulnerability, and who will often carry the heaviest leadership responsibilities.

In business, these might be co-founders, top managers, or senior advisors. Don't try to treat everyone at the same level of intimacy. Go deep with a few, and they will help carry the weight of leadership.

Empowering and Releasing

One of the greatest mistakes leaders make is keeping all responsibility to themselves. They fear delegation will dilute their control, but refusing to release responsibility suffocates growth.

Jesus gave His disciples authority (Luke 9:1–2). He sent them out to preach, heal, and deliver—even before they were fully mature. He trusted them enough to release power into their hands. Yes, they made mistakes. But those mistakes became part of their training.

In business, empower your team with real authority. Let them make decisions, represent the brand, and lead initiatives. Correct them when necessary, but don't micromanage. Empowerment creates ownership, and ownership fuels multiplication.

Building a Team Culture

Your core team must embody the culture of your brand. If culture is not intentionally shaped, it will form by accident—and often in unhealthy ways.

Steps to build strong team culture:

- Define Core Values. Write them down clearly. For example: integrity, service, innovation, excellence.
- Live the Values. Team members will follow what you do, not just what you say.
- Celebrate Wins. Publicly honor team members who embody the culture.
- Correct Quickly. Don't let violations of culture slide. Jesus rebuked His disciples when they argued about who was greatest (Luke 22:24–26). Correction protects culture.

Preparing for Succession

The real test of your leadership is what happens when you're not in the room. If everything falls apart without you, you haven't built a team—you've built dependence. Jesus prepared His disciples to carry the mission after His ascension. That's why the movement grew exponentially after He left.

In business, plan for succession. Train others to lead so that your vision can outlast you. A strong team ensures continuity, legacy, and long-term growth.

Action Steps for Building Your Core Team

1. Identify 5–12 People who show alignment, character, and commitment.
2. Create an Inner Circle of 2–3 to invest in most deeply.
3. Develop a Training Rhythm (weekly or monthly) to reinforce vision and skills.
4. Delegate Real Authority to your team members so they grow in ownership.
5. Build Team Culture by consistently modeling and celebrating your values.
6. Plan for Multiplication so your team can eventually train others.

Conclusion

Jesus' decision to build a core team of Twelve was not a side note—it was central to His strategy. By pouring into a few, He ensured the mission would multiply to many. For leaders and entrepreneurs, the lesson is clear: you don't build movements by carrying everything yourself—you build them by building others.

Your business or mission will rise or fall on the strength of your core team. Choose wisely, invest deeply, empower boldly, and release confidently. When you build a strong "Twelve," you ensure that your vision will not only succeed today but endure for generations.

CHAPTER 7

Servant Leadership: Washing Feet

The Principle — Why True Leadership Begins With Service

The world often paints leadership as power, prestige, and position. Leaders are expected to be the ones at the top, giving orders, receiving honor, and enjoying privilege. But the model Jesus gave us flips this assumption upside down. True leadership is not about how many people serve you—it's about how many people you serve.

This is the essence of servant leadership. The term may sound counterintuitive in a culture that prizes influence and authority, but it is the secret to building lasting impact. Jesus showed us that leadership is not measured by control but by care, not by title but by towel, not by status but by sacrifice.

Why Service Builds Real Influence

Leadership rooted in power often creates compliance but rarely inspires loyalty. People may follow because they have to, but their hearts are not in it. On the other hand, leadership rooted in service creates commitment. When people feel valued, understood, and cared for, they willingly follow.

Think about the leaders who made the biggest difference in your life. Chances are, they weren't the ones who barked orders or flaunted authority. They were the ones who listened, encouraged, supported, and gave of themselves to help you succeed. Service builds trust, and trust builds influence.

This is why servant leadership works. Service disarms pride, dissolves fear, and develops genuine loyalty. People don't remember leaders who demanded respect; they remember leaders who gave respect.

Servant Leadership Versus Self-Serving Leadership

There's a stark difference between servant leadership and self-serving leadership:

- Self-serving leadership says, "I'm here to be recognized."
- Servant leadership says, "I'm here to recognize others."
- Self-serving leadership uses people to build empires.

- Servant leadership uses empires to build people.
- Self-serving leadership protects the leader's comfort.
- Servant leadership sacrifices for the team's growth.

Jesus summarized it perfectly in Matthew 20:25–26: "You know that the rulers of the Gentiles lord it over them, and their high officials exercise authority over them. Not so with you. Instead, whoever wants to become great among you must be your servant."

The Power of Humility

Servant leadership is powered by humility. Humility is not weakness—it is strength under control. A humble leader doesn't think less of themselves; they think of themselves less often. They are not obsessed with proving their worth because they know their worth is secure.

This humility gives leaders freedom. They are free to admit mistakes, free to empower others, free to share credit, and free to lift others up. A prideful leader hoards control; a humble leader multiplies it. That multiplication is what creates movements that outlast the leader.

Servant Leadership in Action

Servant leadership is not theory; it is practice. It is demonstrated in how you treat people when no one is watching. It is shown in small, everyday acts of care, not just in grand gestures.

A servant leader might:

- Stay late to help a team member finish a project.
- Celebrate the wins of others without drawing attention to themselves.
- Listen before speaking, seeking to understand before being understood.
- Take responsibility when things go wrong and share credit when things go right.

Servant leadership is embodied in the posture of asking: "How can I help you succeed?"

Why This Principle Matters in Business

In business, servant leadership creates culture. Employees are not just workers—they are people with dreams, struggles, and potential. When leaders serve their people, the workplace becomes a place of trust and empowerment. Turnover decreases, innovation increases, and loyalty deepens.

Servant leadership also impacts customers. A company that exists to serve rather than exploit creates long-term relationships rather than one-time transactions. Customers sense when a business genuinely cares about their needs, and they reward that care with loyalty and advocacy.

The Paradox of Servant Leadership

Here is the paradox: the more you serve, the greater your influence becomes. Leaders who chase power often lose it, but leaders who give power away gain it back multiplied. Jesus' life illustrates this paradox perfectly. Though He humbled Himself to wash feet, heal the sick, and serve the poor, His influence outlasted kings, emperors, and rulers who demanded recognition.

This principle echoes across history. Leaders who served—like Mother Teresa or Martin Luther King Jr.—are remembered far more than leaders who simply demanded obedience. Their humility became their legacy.

Principle in Practice

To apply this principle in your own leadership:

1. Redefine Success. Stop measuring leadership by how much authority you have. Measure it by how many people you have lifted.
2. Adopt the Towel. Find practical ways to serve your team daily. Service is not abstract; it's tangible.
3. Ask, Don't Assume. Ask your team what they need, instead of assuming you know.
4. Share Credit Generously. Point to others when things go well. Take responsibility when they don't.
5. Stay Accessible. Don't let titles or positions create walls. Stay approachable.

Conclusion

Servant leadership is not a trendy management theory—it is a timeless principle modeled by Jesus. He showed us that the greatest leaders are not those who sit on thrones but those who kneel with towels. Leadership begins with service, and service builds trust, loyalty, and influence that lasts.

If you want to lead like Jesus, start by serving. Influence built on pride will fade, but influence built on humility will endure. In the kingdom of God—and in the marketplace—the greatest leaders are those who serve.

Biblical Insight — Jesus Washing the Disciples' Feet in John 13

If the Gospels give us many images of Jesus as Teacher, Shepherd, and Savior, John 13 gives us one of the most shocking images of Jesus as Servant. On the night before His crucifixion, Jesus did something His disciples never expected: He took off His outer garment, wrapped a towel around His waist, knelt down, and began to wash their feet.

This single act, recorded only in John's Gospel, is one of the clearest demonstrations of what servant leadership looks like in practice. For the disciples, it was scandalous. For us, it is instructive.

The Context of the Foot Washing

To understand the weight of this moment, we must grasp the cultural context. In first-century Palestine, people walked long distances on dusty roads wearing open sandals. By the end of the day, their feet were dirty, sweaty, and often cracked from heat. Washing feet was a necessary task but one reserved for the lowest household servant.

For a rabbi to wash the feet of his disciples was unthinkable. Teachers were held in high regard, and disciples were expected to serve them, not the other way around. Yet on the night when He could have demanded their attention, comfort, and loyalty, Jesus chose instead to serve them in the most humble way possible.

The Act Itself

John 13:3–5 sets the stage:

"Jesus knew that the Father had put all things under his power, and that he had come from God and was returning to God; so he got up from the meal, took off his outer clothing, and wrapped a towel around his waist. After that, he poured water into a basin and began to wash his disciples' feet, drying them with the towel that was wrapped around him."

Notice the connection: Jesus was fully aware of His divine authority ("the Father had put all things under his power"), yet He expressed that authority through humility. He didn't cling to His position—He used it to serve. This is the paradox of leadership in the Kingdom of God: the more secure you are in your identity, the freer you are to serve others.

Peter's Resistance

When Jesus reached Peter, the bold disciple resisted: "Lord, are you going to wash my feet?" (John 13:6). His protest wasn't arrogance—it was shock. For Peter, this was backwards. Rabbis didn't wash disciples' feet. Leaders didn't kneel before followers.

Jesus responded: "You do not realize now what I am doing, but later you will understand" (John 13:7). This shows us that servant leadership often feels upside down in the moment. People don't always recognize the power of humility right away. It is only later, with reflection, that the true impact becomes clear.

When Peter insisted, "You shall never wash my feet," Jesus replied, "Unless I wash you, you have no part with me" (John 13:8). Here Jesus connected service with relationship. To follow Him wasn't just to honor Him as Lord but to accept His humility. Leadership and servanthood were inseparable in His kingdom.

The Lesson for the Disciples

After finishing, Jesus explained:

"Do you understand what I have done for you? ... You call me 'Teacher' and 'Lord,' and rightly so, for that is what I am. Now that I, your Lord and Teacher, have washed your feet, you also should wash one another's feet. I have set you an example that you should do as I have done for you" (John 13:12–15).

The message was clear: leadership is not about being served but about serving. Greatness is not measured by who kneels before you but by whom you are willing to kneel before.

This wasn't just about physical feet washing. It was a metaphor for the posture of the heart. Jesus was teaching them to embody humility, to lower themselves for the sake of others, and to lead not from pride but from love.

Symbolism of the Foot Washing

1. Humility. Jesus demonstrated that true authority is expressed in humility.
2. Cleansing. Washing feet symbolized spiritual cleansing. Just as He washed their feet, He would soon cleanse their hearts through the cross.
3. Service. The towel and basin became symbols of the leader's call to serve.
4. Equality. By washing all the disciples' feet—including Judas, who would betray Him—Jesus showed that

servant leadership extends even to those who oppose or fail us.

The Disciples' Transformation

This act left a lasting impression. The disciples didn't fully grasp it in the moment, but after the resurrection and the coming of the Holy Spirit, the lesson of John 13 became part of the DNA of the early church.

We see echoes of this in their writings:

- Paul wrote, "Do nothing out of selfish ambition or vain conceit. Rather, in humility value others above yourselves" (Philippians 2:3).
- Peter, who once resisted having his feet washed, later instructed leaders: "Be shepherds of God's flock that is under your care, watching over them—not because you must, but because you are willing, as God wants you to be; not pursuing dishonest gain, but eager to serve" (1 Peter 5:2).

The disciples were transformed by Jesus' example. What had shocked them at first became their guiding principle.

Why John Highlights This Scene

Interestingly, John doesn't include the Last Supper institution of bread and wine (as Matthew, Mark, and Luke do). Instead, he gives us the foot washing. Why? Because John wanted to emphasize the heart behind the covenant: service and humility. Jesus' death on the cross was the ultimate act of service, and the foot washing was a foreshadowing of that sacrificial love.

Lessons for Today

From this passage, we learn several timeless lessons about leadership:

1. Authority is not diminished by service; it is displayed through service.
2. Humility is not weakness but strength in action.
3. Leaders must embody the culture they want to create. If you want a culture of service, serve.
4. No one is beneath your care. If Jesus washed Judas's feet, we cannot exclude those who challenge or disappoint us.

Conclusion

John 13 shows us a radically different vision of leadership. In a world where leaders are often elevated above their followers, Jesus lowered Himself below them. In doing so, He redefined greatness. His act of washing feet was not just a moment in history—it was a model for all time.

For the disciples, it was a shocking reversal of expectations. For us, it is an invitation. If we want to lead like Jesus, we must pick up the towel and basin. Leadership is not about climbing higher—it's about stooping lower. True greatness is found not in being served but in serving.

Business Application — Servant Leadership in Modern Organizations

In today's fast-paced, competitive, and often cutthroat business environment, leadership is frequently equated with dominance, authority, and control. Yet history and experience show us that the most effective and enduring leaders are those who lead by serving. This principle, modeled by Jesus in John 13 when He washed His disciples' feet, has direct and transformative application in the marketplace. Servant leadership is not just a spiritual idea—it is a practical framework that produces stronger teams, healthier cultures, and more loyal customers.

Why Servant Leadership Works in Business

Servant leadership builds trust. And trust is the currency of modern business. Employees don't want to work for tyrants; they want to work for leaders who care about them as people. Customers don't want to be treated as numbers; they want to be valued as individuals. Investors don't want to fund hollow organizations; they want to support companies with integrity and vision.

When leaders put people first—when they adopt the posture of service—loyalty, creativity, and growth naturally follow. This is because people flourish in environments where they feel safe, respected, and supported. Servant leaders create those environments.

Shifting the Leadership Paradigm

Most organizations operate under a "top-down" model of leadership: executives give orders, managers enforce them, and employees carry them out. While this can achieve short-term results, it often breeds resentment, disengagement, and high turnover. Servant leadership inverts the pyramid: leaders exist to support their teams, remove obstacles, and empower employees to succeed.

This doesn't mean leaders lose authority. Rather, it means they redefine authority as responsibility. Authority is not about privilege; it's about accountability for the wellbeing of those under your care. Just as Jesus, knowing He had "all power," chose to wash feet, leaders with true authority demonstrate it through service, not domination.

Servant Leadership in Action

So what does servant leadership look like in a modern business context?

1. Active Listening. Servant leaders listen more than they speak. They prioritize understanding employees' concerns, ideas, and needs before making decisions. This builds trust and demonstrates respect.
2. Empowerment. Instead of micromanaging, servant leaders give employees the tools, training, and authority to make decisions. Empowered employees are more engaged, innovative, and loyal.
3. Modeling Values. Servant leaders live the values they expect from others. If integrity, excellence, or humility are part of the company's values, leaders must embody them first.
4. Personal Investment. Servant leaders know their people. They celebrate birthdays, check in during tough seasons, and genuinely care about the wellbeing of their team members. Small gestures build massive loyalty.
5. Shared Success. When wins happen, servant leaders give credit to the team rather than hoarding recognition. This fosters collaboration instead of competition.

The Ripple Effect of Servant Leadership

When leaders serve, the ripple effect spreads across the entire organization:

- Employees Feel Valued. They show up with energy, passion, and ownership because they know they matter.
- Culture Strengthens. Toxicity decreases because humility and respect are modeled from the top.
- Customers Notice. Service to employees translates into service to customers. When employees feel cared for, they naturally care more for clients.
- Innovation Increases. People in servant-led organizations feel safe to share ideas without fear of ridicule, which fosters creativity.
- Turnover Decreases. Loyalty rises because employees don't want to leave environments where they are genuinely respected.

Case Studies of Servant Leadership in Business

- Southwest Airlines. Founder Herb Kelleher embodied servant leadership. He treated employees like family, often working alongside them and putting their wellbeing first. As a result, Southwest built one of the strongest cultures in aviation, and customers felt the difference.

- Starbucks. Howard Schultz built Starbucks not just on coffee but on the idea of creating a "third place" where employees (called partners) and customers alike felt cared for. Servant leadership at the top filtered into customer experience at every level.
- Chick-fil-A. Known for exceptional service, Chick-fil-A trains employees to value guests above transactions. This culture of service, modeled from leadership, makes them stand out in a crowded fast-food market.

Each of these companies demonstrates that servant leadership is not weakness—it is strategic strength.

Servant Leadership and Customer Experience

Servant leadership doesn't stop at internal culture; it extends to customers. Businesses that serve customers with humility and care create memorable experiences that drive loyalty.

For example, consider two scenarios:

- Company A provides a product but offers no follow-up or care. Customers feel like numbers.
- Company B provides the same product but follows up with a thank-you note, checks in to ensure satisfaction, and offers ongoing support. Customers feel valued.

Guess which company earns repeat business and referrals? The one that serves.

Practical Steps to Implement Servant Leadership

1. Redefine Leadership Metrics. Measure success not only by revenue but by employee satisfaction, retention, and customer loyalty.
2. Develop a Service Mindset. Train leaders at all levels to ask, "How can I help you succeed?" rather than "What can you do for me?"
3. Create Feedback Loops. Give employees safe channels to share concerns and ideas. Then act on that feedback.
4. Invest in People Development. Provide training, mentorship, and opportunities for growth. Serving your team includes equipping them for their future.
5. Celebrate Service. Recognize and reward acts of service within your organization to reinforce the culture.

Avoiding Misconceptions

Servant leadership is not about being passive, soft, or indecisive. It is about leading with strength expressed through humility. Servant leaders still make tough decisions, set clear standards, and hold people accountable. But they do so with the heart of a servant, not the pride of a dictator.

Conclusion

In John 13, Jesus showed us that true leadership is not about position but posture. In modern organizations, servant leadership translates into cultures of trust, loyalty, and growth. Leaders who pick up the towel—metaphorically speaking—create environments where people flourish, customers are valued, and businesses endure.

The lesson is timeless: if you want influence that lasts, serve. If you want teams that thrive, serve. If you want customers who return again and again, serve. The greatest leaders, in any field, are those who put others first.

CHAPTER 8

Emotional Intelligence: Weeping Over Jerusalem

The Principle — Why Emotional Intelligence Is Essential for Leadership

In the modern world, intelligence is often measured by IQ—our ability to analyze, calculate, and solve problems. But research and experience show that another form of intelligence often matters more in leadership: emotional intelligence (EQ). While IQ can get you in the door, EQ determines how far you go.

Emotional intelligence is the ability to recognize, understand, and manage your own emotions while also perceiving and responding effectively to the emotions of others. It is about more than "being nice" or "being empathetic"—it is about connecting authentically, navigating conflict, building trust, and making wise decisions under pressure.

Jesus embodied this perfectly. He wasn't emotionally detached, robotic, or distant. He allowed Himself to feel deeply, to express compassion, to experience righteous anger, and to mourn with sincerity. One of the most powerful examples of this is found in Luke 19:41–44, when He wept over Jerusalem. His tears revealed His emotional connection to the people, His awareness of their pain, and His heartbreak over their blindness to truth. That moment wasn't weakness—it was strength rooted in love.

Why Emotional Intelligence Matters in Leadership

Leadership is not only about strategy and execution. It's about people. And people are emotional beings. Leaders who ignore emotions—either their own or those of others—inevitably damage trust, create resentment, and weaken relationships. On the other hand, leaders who develop emotional intelligence foster loyalty, collaboration, and long-term success.

Consider these realities:

- Employees don't quit companies—they quit managers. Often, the reason isn't incompetence but a lack of emotional intelligence: poor communication, lack of empathy, or inability to manage conflict.

- Customers don't just buy products—they buy experiences. Those experiences are shaped not only by efficiency but by emotional connection.
- Teams don't thrive on pressure alone—they thrive when leaders can inspire confidence, calm anxiety, and encourage resilience.

Emotional intelligence bridges the gap between vision and people. Without it, leaders may have clear goals but no followers willing to pursue them.

The Components of Emotional Intelligence

Psychologists often break EQ into four core components:

1. Self-Awareness. Recognizing your own emotions, triggers, strengths, and weaknesses. Leaders who lack self-awareness often misread situations and project frustration onto others.
2. Self-Management. The ability to control impulses, manage stress, and act with patience rather than reaction. Emotional regulation separates leaders from tyrants.
3. Social Awareness. The capacity to sense the emotions of others, to read a room, and to understand what people are feeling beyond their words.
4. Relationship Management. Using emotional insight to build trust, resolve conflicts, and inspire others.

Jesus demonstrated all four. He knew His emotions (weeping over Jerusalem), controlled them (remaining silent before Pilate), sensed others' needs (compassion for the hungry crowds), and built relationships that turned fishermen into world-changers.

Emotional Intelligence vs. Emotional Suppression

Many leaders mistakenly believe that showing emotion is weakness. They suppress their feelings, thinking that stoicism equals strength. But suppression is not the same as intelligence. Suppressed emotions often explode later in unhealthy ways—anger, burnout, or detachment.

Emotional intelligence doesn't deny emotions; it acknowledges them and uses them wisely. Jesus didn't hide His feelings. He openly expressed joy, sorrow, compassion, and even frustration. His emotions were real, yet they were always aligned with purpose. That is true emotional intelligence: emotions that serve the mission rather than sabotage it.

Why Leaders Must Develop Emotional Intelligence

1. Trust. People trust leaders who are authentic. When you express real concern, people know you care.
2. Clarity. Leaders with EQ can read unspoken tensions, allowing them to address issues before they escalate.

3. Resilience. EQ helps leaders regulate stress and stay steady under pressure, which reassures teams.
4. Influence. People are more likely to follow leaders who connect emotionally than those who remain detached.

Without EQ, leaders may succeed in the short term but fail in the long term. They may win battles but lose people. With EQ, leaders inspire both results and relationships.

The Example of Jesus' Tears

When Jesus wept over Jerusalem, He showed us that leadership requires more than vision—it requires heart. He wasn't just lamenting a city's failure; He was showing deep empathy for people who didn't understand the consequences of their choices. His tears revealed love, not weakness.

In that moment, Jesus modeled what every leader must learn: caring deeply for people even when they disappoint you. Leaders with EQ don't detach themselves from pain—they allow compassion to guide their response.

Principle in Practice

If you want to grow in emotional intelligence as a leader:

1. Pause Before Reacting. When emotions rise, take a breath before responding. Reaction breeds regret; reflection breeds wisdom.
2. Name Your Emotions. Don't just say "I'm fine." Be honest with yourself: frustrated, tired, hopeful, anxious. Naming emotions gives you power over them.
3. Practice Empathy. Ask, "What might this person be feeling?" not just "What are they saying?"
4. Listen Beyond Words. Body language, tone, and silence often reveal more than speech.
5. Respond With Compassion. Even when correction is needed, lead with care, not condemnation.

Conclusion

The principle of emotional intelligence is clear: leadership is not just about thinking—it's about feeling. Strategy without empathy creates cold organizations. Vision without compassion creates disconnected leaders. But when leaders combine clarity of thought with depth of feeling, they create influence that transforms people as well as results.

Jesus' tears over Jerusalem show us that emotional connection is not weakness but strength. It is the mark of leaders who care deeply, who see clearly, and who love fully. If you want to lead like Jesus, don't just sharpen your mind—tenderize your heart. Emotional intelligence is the secret ingredient that makes leadership human, relatable, and enduring.

Biblical Insight — Jesus Weeping Over Jerusalem and Other Displays of Emotion in the Gospels

When we look at Jesus in the Gospels, we see a leader who was not emotionally detached or aloof but one who engaged deeply with human experience. His ability to feel, express, and direct emotion with purpose shows us that He was the ultimate model of emotional intelligence. He wasn't ruled by His emotions, nor did He suppress them. Instead, He integrated them into His mission, allowing love, compassion, and even grief to guide His actions.

One of the clearest examples of this is in Luke 19:41–44, where Jesus weeps over Jerusalem. This moment, alongside other recorded displays of His emotions, reveals His heart and provides a blueprint for how leaders can embrace emotional intelligence as part of their calling.

Jesus Weeping Over Jerusalem (Luke 19:41–44)

As Jesus approached Jerusalem on what we now call Palm Sunday, the crowd cheered Him with shouts of "Hosanna!" waving palm branches and celebrating Him as King. Yet as

He drew near the city, His heart broke. Luke writes: "As he approached Jerusalem and saw the city, he wept over it and said, 'If you, even you, had only known on this day what would bring you peace—but now it is hidden from your eyes'" (Luke 19:41–42).

This is a profound picture of emotional intelligence at work. Jesus wasn't caught up in the adoration of the crowds. He wasn't blinded by celebration. He saw deeper. He discerned the true state of Jerusalem—not its applause, but its spiritual blindness. His tears revealed a leader who could hold both triumph and tragedy in tension.

This moment shows us:

- Awareness. Jesus was aware of His own emotions and did not hide them.
- Empathy. He felt the pain of others, even those who would reject Him.
- Clarity. He could see beyond appearances to the reality of the situation.
- Purpose. His emotions aligned with His mission, not against it.

His tears were not weakness but wisdom—a recognition of the cost of rebellion and the grief of missed opportunity.

Jesus Weeping at Lazarus's Tomb (John 11:35)

The shortest verse in the Bible is also one of the most profound: "Jesus wept." When His friend Lazarus died, Jesus was surrounded by mourning family and friends. Even though He knew He would raise Lazarus from the dead, He allowed Himself to feel the weight of their grief. He didn't bypass their emotions with premature solutions—He entered their pain.

This shows us that emotional intelligence doesn't always rush to fix things. Sometimes it pauses to feel, to mourn, to connect. Jesus' tears at Lazarus's tomb demonstrate empathy at its fullest: stepping into another's sorrow even when you know the ending.

Jesus' Compassion for the Crowds

Repeatedly, the Gospels record that Jesus was "moved with compassion" when He saw the crowds (e.g., Matthew 9:36, Matthew 14:14). He didn't see people as numbers, interruptions, or obstacles. He saw their hunger, sickness, confusion, and weariness. His emotional intelligence allowed Him to perceive unspoken needs and respond with care.

For example, before feeding the 5,000, the text says, "When Jesus landed and saw a large crowd, he had compassion on them and healed their sick" (Matthew 14:14). His compassion guided His actions. Instead of sending them away, He fed them.

His ability to sense their need led to a miracle that satisfied thousands.

Jesus' Righteous Anger in the Temple

Emotional intelligence does not mean suppressing all negative emotion. It means directing emotion in alignment with values. Jesus displayed righteous anger when He drove out the money changers from the temple (Matthew 21:12–13). His anger wasn't reckless or selfish—it was purposeful. He wasn't losing control; He was exercising control on behalf of justice and reverence for God's house.

This shows us that leaders with emotional intelligence are not emotionless. They feel anger but channel it into constructive, purposeful action rather than destructive outbursts.

Jesus' Grief in Gethsemane

In Matthew 26:37–38, as Jesus entered Gethsemane, He told His disciples: "My soul is overwhelmed with sorrow to the point of death. Stay here and keep watch with me." He didn't hide His vulnerability. He named His emotion—sorrow—and invited His closest friends into His pain.

This moment demonstrates transparency. A lesser leader might have pretended to be strong, masking emotions to maintain an image of invincibility. Jesus modeled the opposite: honesty about emotional struggle while still submitting to God's will.

That combination of vulnerability and strength is a hallmark of true EQ.

What These Examples Teach Us

From these snapshots of Jesus' life, we learn several lessons about emotional intelligence:

1. Feel Deeply Without Being Controlled. Jesus allowed Himself to feel but never let emotions derail His mission. His tears and anger served truth.
2. Empathy Is Central to Leadership. Whether mourning with Mary and Martha or weeping over Jerusalem, Jesus entered into others' pain. Leaders who empathize connect more deeply with those they serve.
3. Vulnerability Builds Trust. Jesus wasn't afraid to show sorrow. His openness in Gethsemane showed His disciples that strength and honesty can coexist.
4. Emotions Can Propel Action. Compassion moved Jesus to heal. Anger moved Him to cleanse the temple. Emotion wasn't a distraction—it was a catalyst for mission.
5. True EQ Balances Head and Heart. Jesus could see the larger mission (the cross, resurrection, Kingdom) while still honoring present emotions.

Why the Gospels Highlight Emotion

The Gospel writers could have portrayed Jesus as stoic, detached, and superhuman in a way that denied emotion. But they chose to highlight His tears, compassion, and sorrow. Why? Because emotions reveal His humanity and His heart.

John emphasizes His tears at Lazarus's tomb. Luke highlights His lament over Jerusalem. Matthew and Mark describe His sorrow in Gethsemane. These details were not incidental—they were essential. They showed that the Savior of the world was also a man who felt deeply, loved fully, and cared personally.

Conclusion

Jesus' emotional displays in the Gospels are not signs of weakness—they are signs of wisdom. His tears, His compassion, His righteous anger, and His sorrow all reveal a leader fully in touch with both His mission and the people He came to serve.

For us, these examples serve as both comfort and challenge. Comfort, because we see that God understands our emotions—He has felt them Himself. Challenge, because we are called to lead like Jesus: with awareness, empathy, vulnerability, and compassion.

When we weep over our "Jerusalem"—whether that is a team, a company, a family, or a community—we are embodying the heart of Christ. Emotional intelligence is not optional for leaders; it is the very essence of Christlike leadership.

Business Application — Emotional Intelligence in Leadership and Organizations

In the modern marketplace, emotional intelligence (EQ) is one of the most sought-after qualities in leadership. Studies repeatedly confirm that leaders with high EQ outperform those with high IQ but low emotional awareness. In fact, many organizations now rank EQ above technical skills when hiring for leadership positions because they know: business is about people, and people are emotional.

If you want to influence others, build loyal teams, and inspire long-term commitment, you must do more than think clearly—you must feel deeply and respond wisely. Jesus' example of weeping over Jerusalem demonstrates the heart every leader needs: the ability to see beyond the surface, connect with people's struggles, and act from compassion. Let's explore how this translates directly into business.

Why Emotional Intelligence Matters for Organizations

1. Trust and Loyalty. Employees are more loyal to leaders who understand and care about them. Customers are more loyal to brands that connect emotionally, not just functionally.

2. Conflict Resolution. EQ enables leaders to navigate tension, mediate disagreements, and create harmony. Without it, conflicts fester and destroy culture.
3. Resilience Under Pressure. Leaders with EQ regulate stress and model calmness. Teams mirror this steadiness, especially in crisis.
4. Engagement and Performance. Studies show employees led by high-EQ managers are more engaged, innovative, and productive. Why? Because emotional intelligence creates safety and motivation.

In short: IQ may open opportunities, but EQ sustains them.

Core Skills of EQ in Business

To apply emotional intelligence in an organizational setting, leaders must intentionally cultivate four skills:

1. Self-Awareness

Great leaders know themselves. They are honest about their strengths, weaknesses, triggers, and emotional tendencies. For example, a leader who knows they get impatient in stressful meetings can prepare by slowing down and asking clarifying questions rather than snapping at the team.

Practical Tip: Keep a leadership journal. After difficult interactions, write down what you felt, why you felt it, and how you responded. This builds emotional clarity.

2. Self-Management

It's not enough to recognize emotions—you must regulate them. Leaders with EQ don't let stress, anger, or fear drive reckless decisions. They pause, breathe, and respond thoughtfully.

Practical Tip: Develop a "pause practice." Before sending an email or making a decision under stress, wait 24 hours if possible. This reduces reactionary mistakes.

3. Social Awareness

This is the ability to read a room, sense unspoken dynamics, and recognize others' emotions. Jesus excelled at this. He knew when the crowd was hungry, when the disciples were afraid, and when individuals were hurting.

Practical Tip: In meetings, observe body language and tone. Ask open-ended questions like, "How's everyone feeling about this plan?" Don't just look for agreement—look for hesitation or concern.

4. Relationship Management

Finally, EQ means using emotional insight to build and maintain strong relationships. This includes resolving conflicts, inspiring people, and encouraging collaboration. Leaders with high EQ don't just manage projects—they shepherd people.

Practical Tip: Make it a habit to check in with team members not only about work but about life. A two-minute question—

"How are you doing outside of work?"—can build trust that lasts for years.

EQ and Customer Experience

Emotional intelligence isn't just for internal leadership—it's essential for customer relationships. Customers don't just buy products; they buy experiences. Those experiences are shaped by emotion.

- Empathy Creates Loyalty. When customers feel understood, they return. For example, a company that listens empathetically to complaints and responds with care earns more loyalty than one that dismisses feedback.
- Emotion Shapes Decisions. Research shows most purchasing decisions are driven by emotion, not logic. Leaders with EQ design marketing and service around how customers feel, not just what they think.
- Personalization Builds Connection. Businesses that remember customer names, preferences, and past experiences show emotional awareness. This builds trust and repeat business.

How EQ Transforms Workplace Culture

A workplace without emotional intelligence is cold, transactional, and draining. People may show up for a paycheck, but they rarely give their best. A workplace with EQ, however, becomes life-giving.

- Communication Improves. Teams speak honestly and respectfully, rather than bottling up frustrations.
- Innovation Thrives. People feel safe to share ideas without fear of ridicule.
- Retention Rises. Employees stay where they feel valued. Servant leadership and EQ reduce costly turnover.
- Collaboration Deepens. Teams with emotionally intelligent leaders trust each other more and compete less.

The difference is stark: EQ creates cultures people want to be part of.

Practical Action Steps for Leaders

1. Practice Active Listening. In every conversation, focus on the other person's words, tone, and emotions. Reflect back what you hear: "It sounds like you're concerned about…"
2. Respond With Compassion. Even in correction, lead with care. Instead of saying, "You failed," say, "I know this was hard. Let's figure out how to do better next time."

3. Develop Empathy Muscles. Spend time with your team outside of work context. Learn about their families, hobbies, and challenges.
4. Lead With Transparency. Be honest about your own struggles. Vulnerability doesn't weaken authority—it strengthens it.
5. Celebrate Emotions. Don't just reward results; celebrate resilience, perseverance, and teamwork. This validates the emotional journey, not just the outcome.

Avoiding Common EQ Pitfalls

- Over-Emotional Leadership. EQ doesn't mean making every decision based on feelings. It means integrating emotion with wisdom. Leaders must balance empathy with accountability.
- Performative Empathy. People can sense when empathy is fake. Authenticity is non-negotiable.
- Ignoring Self-Care. Leaders with high EQ must also manage their own emotional health. You can't pour into others if your own tank is empty.

Conclusion

Jesus' tears over Jerusalem show us that the greatest leaders don't just think—they feel. They recognize the weight of people's pain, the cost of lost opportunities, and the urgency of compassion. In modern organizations, this translates into emotional intelligence: the ability to understand, regulate, and leverage emotions for the good of people and mission.

Leaders who develop EQ don't just achieve goals; they inspire loyalty. They don't just manage tasks; they build trust. They don't just lead organizations; they transform cultures.

In a world hungry for authentic leadership, emotional intelligence is not optional—it is essential. If you want to lead like Jesus, learn to see with your mind, feel with your heart, and act with compassion. That is the kind of leadership that changes lives and endures for generations.

CHAPTER 9

Handling Opposition: Engaging Pharisees and Critics

The Principle — Why Leaders Must Learn to Handle Opposition

Every leader, whether in ministry, business, or community, will face opposition. Vision always attracts resistance. Success always draws critics. Influence always provokes envy. It's not a matter of if—it's a matter of when. That's why handling opposition wisely is not optional for leaders; it's essential.

Opposition comes in many forms: skeptics who question your credibility, rivals who compete for attention, customers who complain, employees who resist change, or even friends and family who doubt your calling. If you are not prepared to engage opposition, you will either collapse under criticism or become combative and lose credibility. Both extremes destroy influence.

Jesus faced constant opposition throughout His ministry. The Pharisees, Sadducees, scribes, and teachers of the law regularly challenged Him. They tried to trap Him with questions, discredit Him before crowds, and ultimately sought to destroy Him. Yet Jesus never allowed opposition to derail His mission. He responded with wisdom, courage, and restraint. His example shows us that the way you handle critics is just as important as the way you handle followers.

Why Opposition Is Inevitable

1. Vision Threatens Comfort. Leaders disrupt the status quo. Critics often resist because change challenges their comfort zones.
2. Success Provokes Envy. When you grow, others may feel threatened. Opposition often arises not from what you're doing wrong but from what you're doing right.
3. Truth Confronts Power. When leaders speak truth, it exposes corruption, hypocrisy, or mediocrity. Those benefiting from the old system push back.
4. Visibility Attracts Scrutiny. The more visible your platform, the more people will feel free to critique it.

Jesus warned His disciples of this reality: "If the world hates you, keep in mind that it hated me first" (John 15:18). Opposition is not evidence of failure—it's evidence of impact.

The Dangers of Mishandling Opposition

Many leaders fail not because of the opposition itself but because of how they handle it. There are two common extremes:

1. Avoidance. Some leaders fear criticism so much that they shrink back, compromise vision, or quit altogether. In doing so, they silence their influence.
2. Aggression. Other leaders overreact to criticism, lashing out at opponents and alienating potential allies. They may win arguments but lose respect.

Neither approach reflects true leadership. Avoidance leads to irrelevance; aggression leads to isolation. The wise leader learns to face opposition without fear and respond without hostility.

The Balance: Strength With Restraint

Jesus demonstrated a perfect balance: He was firm yet gracious, bold yet wise. He never avoided confrontation, but He also never let anger control Him. His strength was always under restraint.

This balance is the key to handling critics:

- Courage. Speak truth boldly, even when it's unpopular.
- Wisdom. Choose battles carefully; not every critic deserves your energy.
- Restraint. Don't let ego drive your response. Stay mission-focused.

Proverbs 15:1 reminds us: "A gentle answer turns away wrath, but a harsh word stirs up anger." Leaders who master this balance gain influence not by silencing critics but by outlasting them.

Seeing Opposition as Opportunity

Critics can actually serve a purpose:

- They clarify your message. Opposition forces you to articulate your vision more clearly.
- They strengthen your resolve. Facing resistance builds resilience.
- They expose weaknesses. Sometimes critics point out blind spots that need correction.
- They expand your platform. The more opponents challenge you publicly, the more visibility you gain to share your message.

When handled correctly, opposition can become a stepping stone rather than a stumbling block.

Principle in Practice

To handle opposition effectively as a leader:

1. Expect It. Don't be surprised when critics arise. Anticipate resistance as part of leadership.
2. Discern Motives. Some critics are malicious; others are constructive. Learn to distinguish between the two.
3. Stay Mission-Focused. Don't let criticism distract you from purpose. Ask, "Does this concern threaten the mission or just my pride?"
4. Respond, Don't React. Take time before answering critics. A measured response carries more weight than a quick reaction.
5. Use Opposition for Growth. Ask, "What can I learn from this?" Even hostile voices can sharpen your perspective.

Conclusion

The principle is clear: leaders must learn to handle opposition with wisdom, courage, and restraint. Criticism is inevitable, but collapse or combativeness is optional. By following Jesus' example, we can face critics without fear and respond without hostility.

Your ability to handle opposition will define the sustainability of your influence. Followers may celebrate you, but critics will test you. If you want to lead like Jesus, don't fear opposition—use it as an opportunity to clarify vision, grow in resilience, and demonstrate integrity.

Biblical Insight — How Jesus Engaged Pharisees and Critics in the Gospels

The Gospels present us with a recurring theme: Jesus in conflict with the religious leaders of His day—the Pharisees, Sadducees, scribes, and teachers of the law. These groups were powerful, respected, and deeply entrenched in the cultural and religious life of Israel. Yet, rather than welcoming the Messiah they claimed to await, many of them opposed Him fiercely.

For us as leaders, their opposition to Jesus is not only historical detail—it's a divine case study in how to deal with critics. Jesus faced traps, accusations, and confrontations. Sometimes He answered directly, other times He told parables, sometimes He flipped the script with a question, and other times He stayed silent. Each response carried wisdom, restraint, and purpose. Let's explore how Jesus engaged critics in ways that provide timeless lessons for us today.

Opposition Rooted in Threat

Why were the Pharisees and other leaders so hostile toward Jesus? Because His presence threatened their power, prestige, and control. He exposed their hypocrisy, challenged their traditions, and undermined their influence with the people.

Mark 11:18 notes, "The chief priests and the teachers of the law heard this and began looking for a way to kill him, for they feared him, because the whole crowd was amazed at his teaching." Their resistance was not primarily theological—it was political and personal. Opposition often arises when people feel threatened, not simply when they disagree.

Jesus Answering Traps With Wisdom

Repeatedly, critics tried to trap Jesus with trick questions.

- Taxes to Caesar (Matthew 22:15–22). The Pharisees and Herodians asked whether it was lawful to pay taxes to Caesar. If He said yes, He'd alienate the Jews. If He said no, He'd be reported to Rome. Jesus answered: "Give back to Caesar what is Caesar's, and to God what is God's." With one sentence, He silenced His critics and reframed the issue around allegiance to God.
- The Woman Caught in Adultery (John 8:1–11). Critics tried to trap Him between the Law of Moses (which demanded stoning) and Roman law (which restricted executions). Instead of being cornered, Jesus turned the spotlight back on them: "Let any one of you who is without sin be the first to throw a stone at her." One by one, they left.

These examples show Jesus' ability to discern the heart behind the question. He refused to be manipulated into false choices.

Jesus Using Questions to Redirect

One of Jesus' most common tactics with critics was to respond with questions.

- In Matthew 21:23–27, when the chief priests asked, "By what authority are you doing these things?" Jesus replied by asking about John the Baptist's authority. When they refused to answer, He exposed their hypocrisy.
- In Luke 10:25–37, a lawyer tested Him with the question, "What must I do to inherit eternal life?" Instead of giving a lecture, Jesus asked, "What is written in the Law? How do you read it?" Then He told the parable of the Good Samaritan, which turned the questioner's challenge into a lesson.

By using questions, Jesus redirected attention away from traps and onto deeper truths.

Jesus Confronting Hypocrisy Boldly

At times, Jesus responded to critics not with gentle reasoning but with sharp confrontation. In Matthew 23, He delivered a series of "woes" against the Pharisees, calling them hypocrites, blind guides, and whitewashed tombs. This was not personal insult—it was prophetic rebuke. Their hypocrisy was harming people, and Jesus exposed it publicly.

This teaches us that critics don't always need gentle replies. When opposition is rooted in corruption or abuse of power, courage requires confronting it boldly.

Jesus Remaining Silent

Interestingly, there were also times when Jesus chose silence. Before Pilate, when falsely accused, He remained quiet (Matthew 27:14). In other cases, He ignored critics entirely and focused on His mission.

This shows that wisdom is knowing when not to answer. Not every critic deserves your time or energy. Silence can be more powerful than debate when the opposition is insincere.

Jesus Showing Grace Even to Opponents

One of the most surprising aspects of Jesus' interactions with critics is that He still extended grace. He ate with Pharisees (Luke 7:36). He engaged Nicodemus (John 3) in a deep conversation about being born again. Even when confronting, His ultimate goal was redemption, not destruction.

This balance—truth with grace—is central. Leaders must not only expose falsehood but also leave room for repentance and transformation.

Lessons for Leaders From Jesus' Engagement With Critics

1. Discern Motives. Not every question is sincere. Learn to recognize traps versus genuine inquiry.
2. Stay Mission-Focused. Jesus never allowed critics to derail Him. He always tied His answers back to the Kingdom.
3. Use Wisdom in Responses. Sometimes answer directly, sometimes with questions, sometimes with silence. Adapt to the situation.
4. Confront When Necessary. Don't shy away from exposing hypocrisy, but do so with integrity, not ego.
5. Hold Grace and Truth Together. Critics are not just obstacles—they are people God loves. Treat them accordingly.

Conclusion

The Gospels show us a Savior who engaged opposition with unmatched wisdom. He faced traps with clarity, redirected with questions, confronted hypocrisy boldly, remained silent when appropriate, and extended grace even to opponents. His example proves that how you handle critics says as much about your leadership as how you handle supporters.

For leaders today, the lesson is this: opposition is inevitable, but destruction is not. If you respond with the wisdom, restraint, and grace of Jesus, critics can become opportunities to clarify vision, expose truth, and even transform lives.

Business Application — Handling Critics, Competitors, and Opposition in the Marketplace

If Jesus faced opposition from religious leaders while doing good—healing the sick, feeding the hungry, raising the dead—then no leader or entrepreneur today should expect to avoid critics. In business, opposition is guaranteed. It might come from dissatisfied customers, aggressive competitors, skeptical investors, resistant employees, or even friends and family who don't understand your vision. How you handle these voices often determines the longevity and strength of your leadership.

The good news is this: opposition is not inherently bad. In fact, it can be one of the greatest forces for growth, innovation, and influence—if you handle it correctly. Let's explore how to engage critics and competitors with wisdom, courage, and restraint, applying the model of Jesus in the marketplace.

Why Opposition in Business Is Inevitable

1. Disruption Creates Resistance. If your product, service, or idea challenges the status quo, expect pushback. Just as Jesus disrupted religious norms, innovative businesses disrupt industries. Uber faced lawsuits, Netflix faced skepticism, and Amazon faced

ridicule—yet each thrived by persisting through opposition.

2. Success Attracts Scrutiny. The higher your visibility, the more people will critique you. Small startups fly under the radar, but once growth begins, competitors, regulators, and the public all start watching closely.
3. Change Provokes Fear. Employees and even customers may resist change, not because your vision is wrong, but because it's uncomfortable.

Understanding this reality prepares you not to take opposition personally but to see it as part of leadership.

The Wrong Ways to Handle Opposition

1. Ignoring All Critics. Dismissing every complaint or concern as "hate" prevents growth. Some critics are actually pointing out blind spots you need to address.
2. Fighting Every Critic. On the other extreme, leaders who try to argue with everyone waste time and look insecure.
3. Compromising Core Values. Some leaders bend under pressure, diluting vision to appease opponents. This weakens credibility and mission.

These approaches either weaken your brand or exhaust your energy. Wise leaders learn discernment: which voices to ignore, which to learn from, and which to answer boldly.

Learning From Jesus' Model

Jesus gave us a masterclass in responding to critics:

- Discern Motives. Not every question is sincere. Some are traps. In business, not every critic is malicious—some are confused or hurt. Learn to read intent.
- Answer Wisely. Sometimes He spoke plainly, sometimes with parables, sometimes with silence. Business leaders must also adapt responses to the situation.
- Confront Boldly When Necessary. Just as Jesus called out hypocrisy, leaders must address unethical competitors or internal corruption directly.
- Stay Mission-Focused. Jesus never allowed critics to derail His mission. Likewise, don't let opposition distract you from your purpose.

Turning Criticism Into Growth

Handled wisely, opposition can sharpen your organization.

- Customer Complaints. Instead of reacting defensively, treat them as free market research. Ask, "What can we learn from this?" Some of the best innovations are born from criticism.
- Competitors. Instead of obsessing over rivals, use their opposition to refine your strategy and clarify your unique value.

- Internal Resistance. When employees push back, listen. Sometimes resistance exposes weak communication or flawed processes.

Jesus used traps from Pharisees to teach deeper truths. You can use criticism to improve systems, products, and messaging.

Practical Strategies for Leaders

1. Build Emotional Resilience. Don't let criticism shake your identity. Like Jesus, anchor yourself in purpose so you can respond calmly.
2. Create Feedback Channels. Give customers and employees clear ways to share concerns. This prevents criticism from festering in silence.
3. Differentiate Constructive vs. Destructive Criticism. Some critics want to help; others want to harm. Learn to discern.
4. Choose Your Battles. Not every competitor or critic deserves a response. Save energy for battles that matter.
5. Respond With Grace and Strength. Correct false claims firmly but professionally. Don't let ego drive your response.
6. Stay Transparent. In business, honesty about mistakes builds credibility. Critics lose power when you admit shortcomings before they expose them.

Case Studies of Handling Opposition Well

- Apple. Early critics mocked the iPhone as unnecessary. Steve Jobs didn't argue—he stayed mission-focused. Within a year, Apple redefined the smartphone industry.
- Tesla. Elon Musk has faced relentless criticism—from regulators, media, and competitors. While not perfect in his responses, Tesla has used opposition to refine technology and accelerate growth.
- Local Businesses. Smaller organizations often thrive by turning critics into advocates—listening closely, correcting issues, and demonstrating humility.

These examples show that handling opposition with vision and resilience often transforms criticism into credibility.

Action Steps for the Marketplace

1. List Your Likely Opponents. Who might resist your growth—competitors, regulators, skeptical clients? Prepare responses in advance.
2. Clarify Your Core Mission. When criticism arises, measure it against your purpose. If it challenges your mission, address it. If it attacks your ego, ignore it.
3. Train Your Team. Equip employees to respond to customer complaints with empathy and professionalism. Your team's responses shape your reputation.

4. Develop a Crisis Plan. Prepare for public opposition—a bad review going viral, a competitor's smear campaign, or media scrutiny. Leaders who plan ahead stay calm under pressure.
5. Leverage Opposition for Visibility. Sometimes critics unintentionally amplify your message. Use moments of opposition as opportunities to clarify what you stand for.

Conclusion

Opposition in the marketplace is not proof of failure but of impact. The question is not whether you will face critics—it's whether you will face them with wisdom. Jesus showed us how: discern motives, stay focused on mission, and respond with courage, grace, and restraint.

For modern leaders, this means embracing criticism as opportunity, addressing unethical opposition firmly, and never letting detractors derail vision. Critics can sharpen your message, competitors can refine your strategy, and opposition can expand your platform—if you respond like Christ.

Great leaders are not those who avoid opposition but those who outlast it. If you want to build something that endures, don't fear your critics—thank them. They are often the very thing that will push you to grow stronger, lead wiser, and stand firmer.

CHAPTER 10

Strategic Timing: "My Hour Has Not Yet Come"

The Principle — Why Timing Is as Important as Vision

Vision is essential for leadership. Without vision, there is no direction, no motivation, and no future. But vision alone is not enough. Even the clearest vision will fail if pursued at the wrong time. This is where the principle of strategic timing comes into play.

Timing is one of the most overlooked aspects of leadership and business. Many great ideas die, not because they were wrong, but because they were rushed. Others stagnate because leaders waited too long to act. Timing is the bridge between vision and execution.

Jesus understood this principle deeply. Throughout His ministry, He often spoke about His "hour" — a phrase He used to describe the divinely appointed time for His ultimate mission: the cross, resurrection, and the redemption of humanity. On multiple occasions, people tried to accelerate His timeline. They wanted Him to reveal His power, declare Himself as king, or act according to their expectations. But He consistently responded, "My hour has not yet come."

This principle reminds us that success is not just about doing the right thing—it's about doing the right thing at the right time.

Why Timing Matters

1. Premature Action Can Sabotage Success.
   Launching too early can kill momentum. A product that isn't ready, a leader who isn't prepared, or a team that hasn't matured will collapse under pressure.

2. Delayed Action Can Miss Opportunity.
   On the other hand, waiting too long can mean missing windows of opportunity. Markets shift, competitors move in, and interest fades.

3. Timing Balances Preparation With Opportunity.
   Great leaders learn to balance the discipline of preparation with the courage of action. They neither rush nor procrastinate.

The Dangers of Impatience

Impatience is one of the greatest threats to leaders. Driven by pressure, insecurity, or comparison, leaders often want results now. But rushing often leads to regret.

Consider a farmer. If he plants too early, frost will kill the crop. If he plants too late, the harvest won't mature. The farmer's success depends not on his ambition but on his ability to discern seasons. Leaders are the same: discernment of timing determines fruitfulness.

The Dangers of Passivity

Just as dangerous as impatience is passivity. Some leaders wait endlessly for "perfect conditions" that never come. Ecclesiastes 11:4 warns, "Whoever watches the wind will not plant; whoever looks at the clouds will not reap." If you wait for perfection, you'll never act.

Strategic timing doesn't mean inactivity—it means readiness. It means knowing when to move, even if everything isn't perfect, because the season demands action.

Strategic Timing and Alignment

Strategic timing is about alignment—aligning vision with opportunity, preparation with season, and mission with maturity. Leaders who master timing don't simply react to circumstances—they anticipate them. They don't move based on pressure; they move based on principle.

This requires discernment. Discernment is the ability to sense whether the conditions are right—not just in the marketplace but in yourself and your team. Jesus' repeated statement, "My hour has not yet come," shows an acute awareness of divine timing. He knew what to do, but He also knew when to do it.

Timing in Business and Life

In business, timing is everything:

- A product launched too soon flops; launched too late, it's irrelevant.
- An investment made too early drains resources; made too late, it misses growth.
- A conversation held prematurely sparks conflict; held too late, it misses reconciliation.

The same applies to personal life: relationships, career changes, even health decisions hinge on timing. Leaders who fail to master timing often find themselves regretting not just what they did, but when they did it.

How to Develop Strategic Timing

1. Practice Patience. Learn to resist pressure from others. Just because people demand action doesn't mean it's the right time.
2. Prepare Thoroughly. Use waiting seasons to build capacity, strengthen teams, and refine vision.
3. Stay Sensitive. Pay attention to shifts in opportunity, both internal and external. Timing requires awareness.
4. Act Decisively. When the right time comes, don't hesitate. Courage is as important as patience.

The Principle in Summary

Strategic timing means understanding that vision without timing is frustration, and timing without vision is chaos. True leadership requires both. Jesus modeled this by aligning His actions with divine timing, refusing to be rushed or delayed by external pressures.

For leaders today, this principle is a call to discernment. Don't rush ahead of your season, and don't lag behind your opportunity. Learn to sense the timing of your mission and act accordingly.

Conclusion

The principle of strategic timing is simple yet profound: it's not enough to know what to do—you must also know when to do it. Impatience and passivity are both enemies of success. Strategic timing requires patience, preparation, awareness, and decisive action.

If you want to lead like Jesus, don't just focus on vision—focus on timing. Your "hour" will come. The key is to be ready, discerning, and courageous when it does.

Biblical Insight — Jesus' Awareness of Divine Timing in the Gospels

One of the most remarkable qualities of Jesus' ministry was His profound awareness of timing. He was never rushed by the demands of others, never paralyzed by fear of action, and never distracted by false opportunities. Instead, He operated in sync with the Father's will, moving at the right pace and in the right moment. Over and over in the Gospels, we see Jesus speaking of His "hour"—a term He used to describe the appointed time of His suffering, death, resurrection, and ultimate glorification.

By studying these moments, we gain not only theological insight but also practical wisdom for leadership. Jesus teaches us that divine timing is not arbitrary—it is intentional, purposeful, and essential for success.

Jesus at the Wedding in Cana (John 2:1–11)

The first instance of this theme comes in John 2, when Jesus performed His first miracle at the wedding in Cana. When the hosts ran out of wine, Mary approached Him, saying, "They have no more wine." Jesus replied, "Woman, why do you involve me? My hour has not yet come" (John 2:4).

This moment is striking. Jesus had the power to solve the problem immediately, yet He was conscious of timing. His statement reminds us that just because you can do something doesn't mean you should—at least not yet. His reluctance highlights His sensitivity to divine timing. And yet, in obedience to His Father's will, He went on to perform the miracle, turning water into wine and revealing His glory.

This passage shows us that timing often requires discernment between human urgency and divine purpose. Others may pressure you to act, but wisdom comes from knowing when the time is truly right.

Jesus Escaping Premature Arrest

In several places, the Gospels record that Jesus' opponents tried to seize Him, but they could not—because His time had not yet come.

- John 7:30: "At this they tried to seize him, but no one laid a hand on him, because his hour had not yet come."
- John 8:20: "He spoke these words while teaching in the temple courts near the place where the offerings were put. Yet no one seized him, because his hour had not yet come."

These verses show us that timing is not just about human readiness—it's about divine orchestration. Jesus was untouchable until the appointed hour. This reminds leaders that opposition cannot derail you if your season hasn't arrived. Critics may rise, obstacles may appear, but if it's not your time, your mission will not be cut short.

Jesus Aware of the Coming Hour

Later in His ministry, Jesus began to shift His language. Whereas earlier He had said, "My hour has not yet come," He eventually declared, "The hour has come."

- John 12:23: "The hour has come for the Son of Man to be glorified."
- John 13:1: "It was just before the Passover Festival. Jesus knew that the hour had come for him to leave this world and go to the Father."
- John 17:1: "Father, the hour has come. Glorify your Son, that your Son may glorify you."

Jesus lived with acute awareness of timing. He did not resist the hour when it came; He embraced it. This teaches us that waiting for the right time is not about avoidance—it is about readiness. When the moment arrived, Jesus stepped forward with courage, even though it led to suffering.

Timing in Jesus' Ministry Actions

Jesus' sense of timing extended beyond His "hour" of suffering—it also shaped His daily ministry.

1. Withdrawing at the Right Time. When crowds grew too large or hostile, He sometimes withdrew to solitary places (Luke 5:16) or moved on to other towns (Mark 1:38). He understood when to retreat and when to advance.
2. Delaying for Greater Impact. In John 11, when He heard that Lazarus was sick, He delayed two days before going. This was not neglect—it was strategic. His timing ensured that the miracle of raising Lazarus would display God's glory more powerfully.
3. Pacing His Revelation. Jesus often told those He healed not to reveal His identity yet (Mark 1:44, Mark 8:30). Why? Because premature publicity could derail His mission before the appointed time.

Each of these decisions reflects deliberate timing, not random chance.

The Divine Nature of Timing

Jesus' timing was not simply instinct—it was alignment with the Father's will. John 5:19 captures this perfectly: "The Son can do nothing by himself; he can do only what he sees his Father doing, because whatever the Father does the Son also does."

This verse shows us that timing is rooted in intimacy with God. Leaders who want to master timing must cultivate spiritual discernment. Prayer, reflection, and listening to God's direction prepare you to move when the moment is right.

Lessons From Jesus' Timing

From these Gospel accounts, we learn several lessons about divine timing:

1. Not Every Opportunity Is Yours. Just because you can act doesn't mean you should. Timing matters as much as ability.
2. You Are Untouchable Until Your Time Comes. If you are aligned with God's mission, opposition cannot derail you prematurely.
3. Delay Can Be Strategic. Sometimes waiting produces greater impact than acting immediately.
4. When the Time Arrives, Act Boldly. Don't hesitate when your season comes. Courage is required to embrace the hour.

5. Timing Comes From Alignment With God. The more you walk with Him, the clearer His timing becomes.

Conclusion

The Gospels reveal a Savior who lived not only with vision but with timing. He knew when to act, when to wait, when to reveal, when to retreat, and when to embrace His ultimate hour. His awareness of timing ensured that His mission was fulfilled in the right way, at the right moment, with the greatest impact.

For us as leaders, the lesson is profound: discernment of timing is as critical as clarity of vision. If you want to lead like Jesus, don't just ask, "What should I do?" Ask also, "When should I do it?" Timing is the hinge on which destiny swings.

Business Application — Strategic Timing in Leadership and the Marketplace

In business, just like in life, timing is everything. Leaders can have great vision, strong teams, and excellent resources, but if they move at the wrong time, they can sabotage their own success. Strategic timing is the difference between an idea that thrives and one that flops. Jesus' example of being acutely aware of His "hour" provides a blueprint for leaders in the marketplace. His discernment shows us that wisdom is not just knowing what to do but also knowing when to do it.

Why Timing Matters in Business

1. Market Readiness. A product that is introduced before consumers are ready may flop, even if it's brilliant. Likewise, if you wait too long, competitors may seize the opportunity. Think of how Apple's timing with the iPhone reshaped the entire industry.
2. Organizational Readiness. Leaders often rush into expansion without ensuring their team or systems can handle growth. The result? Burnout, customer dissatisfaction, and collapse.
3. Personal Readiness. Sometimes the right opportunity comes, but the leader isn't emotionally or spiritually prepared. Without maturity, success can become a burden rather than a blessing.
4. External Circumstances. Economic shifts, cultural trends, and technological changes all affect timing. Leaders must learn to read the environment just as farmers read the seasons.

In short: the right idea at the wrong time can feel like the wrong idea altogether.

The Dangers of Moving Too Soon

Businesses often fail because leaders act prematurely. They launch before testing, scale before stabilizing, or announce before preparing.

- Startups sometimes rush to market without refining their product, leading to bad reviews that ruin long-term potential.
- Leaders may hire quickly under pressure, bringing on people who don't align with values, creating toxic culture.
- Marketers may push campaigns before understanding customer psychology, wasting resources.

The lesson: impatience is costly. Just as Jesus refused to be rushed into revealing Himself before the appointed time, leaders must resist pressure to act before readiness.

The Dangers of Waiting Too Long

On the other side, many leaders miss opportunities by waiting too long. They overanalyze, second-guess, or stall until the moment passes.

- Blockbuster famously refused to adapt to streaming while Netflix seized the opportunity.
- Kodak invented digital photography but delayed pursuing it, fearing disruption to their film business. The delay cost them their dominance.

Waiting for "perfect conditions" often leads to stagnation. Ecclesiastes 11:4 reminds us: "Whoever watches the wind will not plant; whoever looks at the clouds will not reap." Leaders must act decisively when opportunity aligns with preparation.

Strategic Timing in Decision-Making

How can leaders cultivate better timing? By combining preparation, discernment, and courage.

1. Preparation. Use waiting seasons to refine systems, build teams, and strengthen capacity. Waiting is not wasted if it's used wisely.
2. Discernment. Pay attention to shifts in the market, feedback from customers, and the readiness of your team. Timing requires sensitivity to signals.
3. Courage. When the window opens, move decisively. Strategic timing isn't just about patience—it's about bold action when the moment is right.

Case Studies of Timing in Business

- Amazon. Jeff Bezos waited years before expanding aggressively. Instead of rushing, he reinvested profits to build infrastructure. When the time came, Amazon scaled quickly and sustainably.
- Airbnb. Launched during the 2008 recession, Airbnb thrived because its timing met a cultural and financial need: affordable alternatives to hotels.
- Tesla. Electric vehicles weren't new, but Elon Musk entered the market when cultural concern for sustainability was growing and battery tech was advancing. His timing allowed Tesla to dominate.

These examples show that timing isn't luck—it's awareness, patience, and courage combined.

Strategic Timing With Teams

Strategic timing isn't only about products and markets—it's also about people. Leaders must know when to:

- Promote employees (not too early, not too late).
- Introduce change (before stagnation, but not before readiness).
- Step back themselves (passing the baton at the right moment ensures legacy).

Poor timing in people decisions creates instability. Wise leaders pace development so teams grow at the right speed.

Strategic Timing With Customers

Customers also experience timing. A business that overwhelms customers with too much too soon loses them, while one that responds too late loses trust. Strategic timing means:

- Releasing offers when customers are most receptive.
- Communicating messages when pain points are highest.
- Providing solutions before frustrations become permanent.

For example, gyms strategically market memberships in January when people are motivated for change. Timing aligns product with customer readiness.

Practical Action Steps for Leaders

1. Conduct Timing Reviews. Regularly assess whether your vision is being pursued too quickly or too slowly. Ask: "Is this the right time, or am I being driven by pressure?"
2. Build Market Awareness. Study trends, competitors, and culture. Timing requires watching the environment as carefully as farmers watch the weather.
3. Establish Decision Windows. When opportunities arise, set clear timelines for deciding. Avoid endless delays.
4. Strengthen Your Team During Waiting Seasons. Use times of pause to build systems so you're ready when the door opens.
5. Act Boldly When the Hour Comes. When opportunity aligns with readiness, move quickly and with confidence.

Conclusion

Strategic timing is not guesswork—it is discernment. It requires resisting the urge to rush, avoiding the trap of procrastination, and cultivating the wisdom to move when opportunity and preparation meet.

Jesus modeled this perfectly. He refused to be rushed into action before the right time, but when His hour came, He embraced it fully, even though it led to the cross. His example teaches leaders that success requires more than vision—it requires timing.

In business, the same is true. The wrong move at the wrong time can destroy a good idea, but the right move at the right time can change industries. If you want to lead like Jesus, don't just pray for vision—pray for discernment of timing. Learn to sense your "hour" and act with courage when it arrives.

CHAPTER 11

The Power of Storytelling: Parables as Marketing

The Principle — Why Storytelling Shapes Influence and Persuasion

Human beings are wired for stories. Before there were textbooks, marketing campaigns, or leadership seminars, there were stories passed from one generation to another around fires and in villages. Stories are the oldest form of communication, and they remain the most powerful. Why? Because stories don't just inform the mind—they move the heart. They bypass defenses, stir imagination, and create memory.

Every great leader, teacher, and brand understands this truth: facts tell, but stories sell. You can present endless data, statistics, and logical arguments, but what people remember are the stories you tell. Stories turn abstract ideas into relatable experiences. They give shape and color to values, vision, and purpose.

This principle is why Jesus taught in parables. The Son of God could have delivered lectures filled with theology and philosophy, but He chose instead to wrap divine truths in simple stories of farmers, fishermen, shepherds, seeds, and coins. These everyday pictures carried eternal meaning and connected with audiences across age, class, and culture. His stories were sticky—people repeated them, pondered them, and passed them on.

Why Stories Work

1. Stories Engage Emotion. Logic engages the brain, but stories engage both the brain and the heart. Emotions drive decisions, and stories spark emotions.
2. Stories Are Memorable. Most people forget lectures quickly but can remember a story for years. Stories create mental hooks.
3. Stories Build Connection. A good story helps audiences see themselves in the message. It turns teaching into shared experience.
4. Stories Simplify Complexity. Complex ideas become simple through story. Jesus used parables to explain the Kingdom of God in terms fishermen and farmers could grasp.

5. Stories Spread Easily. Stories are repeatable. A listener can retell a story, passing the message along naturally.

In short, stories multiply influence far faster than data alone.

The Pitfalls of Data Without Story

Modern leaders often fall into the trap of overloading people with information. Presentations are filled with charts, reports, and bullet points. While data has value, information without story is quickly forgotten. Imagine if Jesus had delivered lectures about the structure of heaven using abstract theology alone. Would the crowds have followed Him for days to hear that? Unlikely. Instead, He gave them parables—living metaphors that painted pictures in their minds.

This does not mean we should ignore data. It means we should clothe data in story. Statistics gain power when framed by a human example. A case study with names, faces, and outcomes will always move people more than raw numbers.

Stories and Identity

Stories are also powerful because they shape identity. People don't just buy products or follow leaders—they buy into stories about themselves. Every person wants to see themselves as the hero of their own journey. Leaders who tell stories give people a framework for meaning.

Jesus did this often. In the parable of the Good Samaritan, listeners had to ask themselves: "Who am I in this story? The priest, the Levite, or the Samaritan?" Storytelling forces self-reflection. In business, great brands do the same by telling stories that invite customers to see themselves as overcomers, achievers, or difference-makers.

Storytelling as Multiplication

The beauty of storytelling is that it multiplies. A leader's speech may reach dozens or hundreds, but a story can travel generations. The parables of Jesus have been told, retold, and applied for over two thousand years. They crossed languages, cultures, and centuries because they were more than information—they were story.

This is why great movements are built on narratives, not just strategies. Strategies shift with seasons, but stories endure. A compelling story becomes the anchor of identity for organizations, movements, and communities.

The Discipline of Storytelling

Storytelling is not just art—it is discipline. Leaders must practice crafting stories that:

- Resonate with real life. Use familiar images and examples people understand.

- Point to deeper truth. Don't tell stories for entertainment alone—make them vehicles for meaning.
- Invite reflection. Good stories ask questions rather than forcing conclusions.
- Are repeatable. Keep them simple enough that others can pass them on.

Jesus mastered all four. His parables were simple yet profound, memorable yet mysterious, entertaining yet challenging.

Storytelling in Modern Leadership

In today's world, the most effective leaders use storytelling:

- Entrepreneurs use stories to inspire investors and customers.
- Managers use stories to motivate teams.
- Politicians use stories to rally nations.
- Brands use stories to shape customer identity.

Think of iconic brands like Nike ("Just Do It") or Apple ("Think Different"). They don't just sell products—they sell stories of empowerment and creativity. Their campaigns tap into human identity and aspiration.

Principle in Practice

To practice the principle of storytelling as a leader:

1. Collect Stories. Notice stories in your organization, community, or personal journey that illustrate values and vision.
2. Craft Stories. Practice shaping stories into simple, compelling narratives.
3. Share Stories. Incorporate them into speeches, presentations, and conversations.
4. Repeat Stories. Don't be afraid to tell the same story multiple times—repetition cements identity.
5. Live Stories. Ultimately, the most powerful stories are lived, not just told. Let your life embody the message you speak.

Conclusion

The principle is clear: storytelling is not optional for leaders—it is essential. Stories shape culture, move hearts, and multiply influence. Jesus modeled this by teaching in parables, using simple stories to carry eternal truths.

If you want to lead like Jesus, don't just deliver data—deliver stories. Don't just explain—illustrate. Don't just inform—move. The right story, told at the right time, can outlast a thousand strategies.

Biblical Insight — Jesus' Use of Parables and Storytelling in the Gospels

When we think of Jesus' teaching ministry, one method stands above all others: His use of parables. The Gospels tell us explicitly that Jesus regularly taught the crowds in parables and rarely spoke without them (see Matthew 13:34). Parables were more than illustrations—they were central to His communication strategy. By wrapping eternal truths in simple, relatable stories, Jesus reached ordinary people and left a legacy of teaching that remains unforgettable centuries later.

Why Did Jesus Use Parables?

Several times in the Gospels, Jesus explained why He used parables:

1. Accessibility for the Humble. Parables used everyday imagery—seeds, lamps, coins, sheep—that ordinary listeners could easily grasp. Farmers, fishermen, women in households, and children could all relate. Deep truths were delivered in familiar packages.
2. Challenge for the Proud. While parables clarified truth for those willing to listen, they also concealed truth from the hard-hearted. As Jesus said in Matthew 13:13, "Though seeing, they do not see; though hearing, they do not hear or understand." Parables forced listeners to lean in, ponder, and reflect.
3. Memorability for Generations. A sermon might fade quickly, but a story sticks. Even those who opposed

> Jesus could not ignore His parables. They circulated widely, repeated by the crowds and remembered by His disciples.

Thus, parables were both a gift and a test: a gift to the open-hearted and a test to the resistant.

Examples of Jesus' Parables

The Parable of the Sower (Matthew 13:1–23)

This parable illustrates different responses to God's Word using the image of seeds falling on various types of soil. It resonates because every farmer understood the unpredictability of planting. Yet its deeper meaning—people's varied receptivity to truth—was both convicting and clarifying.

The Parable of the Good Samaritan (Luke 10:25–37)

Told in response to a lawyer's question, this story overturned cultural assumptions. Jews despised Samaritans, yet Jesus made the Samaritan the hero, redefining "neighbor" as anyone in need. This parable is so powerful that it has shaped language and law (think "Good Samaritan laws") to this day.

The Parable of the Lost Sheep, Lost Coin, and Lost Son (Luke 15)

These three parables reveal God's heart for the lost. Each tells of something valuable gone missing and the joy of recovery. By layering images—a shepherd, a woman, and a father—Jesus captured the relentless love of God in ways that theology alone could never communicate.

The Parable of the Mustard Seed (Matthew 13:31–32)

This simple story of a tiny seed growing into a large tree showed how the Kingdom of God starts small but grows into something expansive. Its simplicity hides profound encouragement for anyone discouraged by humble beginnings.

These examples demonstrate Jesus' brilliance as a storyteller. His parables were culturally grounded, emotionally resonant, and spiritually transformative.

The Structure of Jesus' Stories

Jesus' parables followed a consistent pattern that made them effective:

1. Familiar Setting. Something common (a farmer, a shepherd, a housewife).
2. Conflict or Tension. A problem arises (lost sheep, stubborn soil, unjust judge).

3. Resolution. The story resolves with an action or decision.
4. Deeper Truth. A spiritual principle is revealed.

This structure is timeless—it's the same structure used in novels, films, and marketing campaigns today.

Jesus' Parables as Marketing the Kingdom

We might hesitate to use the word "marketing" in a biblical context, but in a sense, Jesus was marketing the Kingdom of God. He was making it attractive, understandable, and compelling to people. He didn't water it down—He packaged it in a way that was accessible.

Instead of preaching abstract concepts like "eschatology" or "soteriology," He spoke of seeds, sheep, lamps, and treasure. He met people where they were, then invited them into deeper truth. This is exactly what effective marketing does: it connects with people's lived experience and shows them something greater.

The Disciples' Response

The disciples often asked Jesus to explain the parables privately (see Mark 4:10–20). This shows two things:

1. Parables invited dialogue and deeper reflection. They weren't meant to be consumed passively.

2. Leadership involves investing extra time in your core team to unpack truths more fully.

By explaining parables privately, Jesus ensured His disciples understood them deeply enough to carry the message forward.

Parables as Sticky Teaching

The genius of parables is their stickiness. A person who heard the story of the prodigal son could retell it to others with little loss of meaning. This made Jesus' message portable. Crowds could carry His teaching beyond His physical presence, spreading it organically.

This is why His message endured. People don't just remember principles; they remember stories. And those stories contain the principles.

Lessons for Leaders

From Jesus' use of parables, leaders today can learn:

1. Use Familiar Language. Speak in terms people understand, not insider jargon.
2. Tell Stories, Not Just Facts. Stories move people in ways information alone cannot.
3. Invite Reflection. Don't spoon-feed every conclusion—let people wrestle with meaning.

4. Make It Memorable. Craft stories that people can easily repeat.
5. Clarify Identity. Use stories to shape how people see themselves.

Conclusion

The Gospels show us that Jesus was not only the Savior of the world but also the greatest storyteller in history. His parables revealed eternal truths in earthly language, reaching hearts and minds alike. They were relatable, memorable, and transformative.

For leaders today, His storytelling method is more than an inspiration—it's a model. If you want to communicate vision, shape culture, and multiply influence, learn to tell stories. Like Jesus, wrap truth in narratives that people can grasp, remember, and share. That is how you spread a message that endures.

Business Application — Storytelling as a Leadership and Marketing Tool in the Modern World

If Jesus—the greatest leader who ever lived—chose storytelling as His primary teaching method, then leaders and entrepreneurs today must not overlook it. Facts may convince, but stories compel. Data may inform, but stories transform. In the marketplace, storytelling is the difference between a product that people forget and a brand that shapes culture.

Modern organizations that thrive don't just sell products; they tell stories. Apple tells a story about creativity and thinking differently. Nike tells a story about personal empowerment and overcoming obstacles. Starbucks tells a story about belonging and creating a "third place" beyond home and work. These companies succeed not because of products alone but because of the narratives that surround them.

For leaders, whether in business, non-profit, ministry, or personal branding, storytelling is one of the most powerful tools available. It attracts attention, builds trust, and multiplies influence.

Why Storytelling Works in Business

1. Stories Humanize Brands. People don't connect deeply with logos or features—they connect with stories of people overcoming challenges, achieving dreams, or serving communities.
2. Stories Make Values Visible. Values like integrity, innovation, or service are abstract until they are embodied in stories of real actions and experiences.
3. Stories Inspire Action. A call to "donate" or "buy" may fall flat. But a story of how one life was changed or one problem was solved compels action.
4. Stories Build Memory. Customers may forget marketing slogans but remember a story that made them laugh, cry, or reflect.

5. Stories Spread Organically. A good story doesn't stay put—it gets repeated, shared, and amplified by others.

Just as Jesus' parables spread from village to village, stories today spread across platforms, multiplying reach.

Storytelling in Leadership

Storytelling is not only for marketing—it's also essential for leadership. Leaders who tell stories shape culture.

- Vision Casting. A leader can present a vision statement, but when they tell a story of what that vision looks like in action, people buy in emotionally.
- Team Motivation. Sharing stories of employees who went above and beyond inspires others to do the same.
- Crisis Management. In times of difficulty, leaders who tell stories of past resilience help teams face present challenges with courage.

Leaders who tell compelling stories invite people to see themselves as part of something larger than themselves.

The Structure of Effective Stories in Business

The same structure Jesus used in His parables works in business storytelling:

1. Relatable Characters. Who is the "main character" of the story? In business, it should often be the customer, not the company.
2. Conflict. Every story needs a problem. What challenge does the customer face?
3. Resolution. How does your product, service, or mission solve that problem?
4. Transformation. What changes after the problem is solved? How does the customer feel?

This simple structure makes messages memorable and compelling.

Examples of Modern Storytelling

- TOMS Shoes. The brand tells the story that every purchase helps someone in need. Customers don't just buy shoes—they buy into generosity.
- Dove's "Real Beauty" Campaign. Instead of just selling soap, Dove tells stories of real women, challenging beauty stereotypes and inspiring confidence.

- Charity: Water. This non-profit doesn't just share statistics about clean water. It tells individual stories of villages transformed when clean water arrives.

Each example shows that stories drive loyalty, advocacy, and lasting impact.

Storytelling Across Platforms

In today's digital world, storytelling happens everywhere:

- Social Media. Short, authentic stories connect faster than polished ads. Instagram reels, TikTok videos, and LinkedIn posts thrive when framed as stories.
- Websites. The "About Us" page should be more than facts—it should tell the story of why the organization exists.
- Emails. Customers are more likely to open and engage with emails that tell stories rather than push sales.
- Public Speaking. Leaders who weave stories into presentations connect with audiences better than those who present dry facts.

The principle is universal: wherever you communicate, lead with story.

Practical Action Steps for Leaders

1. Collect Stories. Build a "story bank" of customer experiences, team wins, and personal lessons. Keep them ready for meetings, marketing, or mentoring.
2. Craft Narratives. Practice shaping these stories with the four-part structure: character, conflict, resolution, transformation.
3. Make Customers the Hero. Position your company as the guide, not the hero. The hero is always the customer whose life is improved.
4. Tell Stories Consistently. Don't just tell stories occasionally—make them part of your culture. Share them in team huddles, marketing materials, and strategy sessions.
5. Live the Story. The most powerful story is authenticity. If your company claims to value service, live it in a way that generates stories of impact.

Avoiding Storytelling Pitfalls

- Exaggeration. Overblown or false stories destroy trust. Authenticity is key.
- Irrelevance. Stories must connect to your audience's reality. If they can't see themselves in the story, they won't care.
- Self-Centeredness. When leaders or brands make themselves the hero, they alienate audiences. The story should highlight the people you serve.

Conclusion

Jesus used storytelling to market the Kingdom of God in a way that ordinary people could grasp, remember, and retell. Today, leaders and businesses can follow His model by using stories to make values visible, vision compelling, and brands memorable.

Storytelling is not a luxury—it is a necessity. In leadership, it builds culture. In marketing, it builds loyalty. In influence, it builds legacy.

If you want to lead like Jesus, learn to tell stories. Wrap truth in narrative, frame vision in parables, and invite people into stories bigger than themselves. The right story can outlive you, outlast your strategy, and multiply your mission for generations.

CHAPTER 12

Excellence in Execution: Feeding the Five Thousand

The Principle — Why Excellence in Execution Multiplies Impact

Ideas inspire, strategies guide, and vision motivates—but none of these matter if execution fails. Leadership is not only about having a great plan; it is about delivering results with consistency and excellence. Many leaders stumble not because their vision is wrong, but because their execution is sloppy. Excellence in execution is what turns potential into reality.

The story of Jesus feeding the five thousand is one of the clearest demonstrations of execution at its finest. Faced with a massive need, limited resources, and an expectant crowd, Jesus didn't panic, compromise, or cut corners. Instead, He organized, blessed, multiplied, and distributed in a way that not only met the need but exceeded it. The miracle reveals a principle every leader and entrepreneur must embrace: excellence in execution turns scarcity into abundance and vision into reality.

Why Execution Matters

1. Vision Without Execution Is Frustration. You can have a brilliant idea, but if you can't deliver, your credibility suffers.
2. Execution Builds Trust. People trust leaders who follow through. Every time you deliver with excellence, you build credibility.
3. Excellence Multiplies Influence. When execution is excellent, word spreads. Customers share positive experiences, and teams rally behind leaders who consistently deliver.
4. Mediocrity Repels. Poor execution doesn't just disappoint—it damages reputation and erodes loyalty.

Execution is not glamorous, but it is essential. It is where strategy meets reality.

The Difference Between Activity and Execution

Many leaders confuse being busy with being effective. Activity fills time; execution produces results. You can attend meetings, draft plans, and brainstorm endlessly—but unless something tangible is delivered with excellence, impact is limited.

Jesus didn't just talk about feeding people—He did it. The miracle of the five thousand shows us that leadership is measured not by intention but by execution.

Excellence Defined

Excellence does not mean perfection. Perfection is unattainable and paralyzing. Excellence means doing the best you can with what you have, paying attention to details, and delivering consistently. Excellence is stewardship—treating resources, people, and opportunities with respect.

Jesus modeled this. He didn't despise the five loaves and two fish. He took them, blessed them, and used them with excellence. The result? Abundance.

Multiplication Through Excellence

Excellence creates multiplication. When people experience excellence, they spread the word, attracting more opportunities and more people. In the miracle, the five thousand weren't just fed—they were satisfied, and there were leftovers. That's the fruit of excellence: overflow.

Why Many Leaders Fail at Execution

1. Lack of Preparation. Poor planning leads to poor delivery.
2. Inattention to Detail. Small details overlooked can ruin great opportunities.
3. Settling for "Good Enough." Leaders who cut corners communicate that mediocrity is acceptable.
4. Failure to Empower. Trying to do everything yourself leads to burnout and inconsistency.

The feeding of the five thousand shows us the opposite: preparation, order, attention, empowerment, and blessing.

The Principle in Practice

To execute with excellence as a leader:

1. Prepare Diligently. Anticipate challenges and plan solutions.
2. Organize Effectively. Bring order to chaos. Jesus had the people sit in groups—order precedes multiplication.
3. Bless What You Have. Don't despise small resources; maximize them.
4. Pay Attention to Quality. Deliver in a way that satisfies, not barely survives.
5. Evaluate and Improve. Collect the leftovers—learn from every effort to steward resources well.

Conclusion

Excellence in execution is what separates dreamers from leaders. The miracle of the five thousand teaches us that scarcity is not an obstacle when resources are stewarded with excellence. Leaders who execute well build trust, multiply influence, and turn vision into reality.

If you want to lead like Jesus, don't just dream big—deliver with excellence. Execution with excellence transforms little into much and creates impact that endures.

Biblical Insight — How Jesus Executed the Feeding of the Five Thousand in the Gospels

The miracle of feeding the five thousand is one of the few miracles recorded in all four Gospels (Matthew 14:13–21, Mark 6:30–44, Luke 9:10–17, and John 6:1–15). Its repetition in Scripture underscores its importance. This wasn't just a display of supernatural power; it was a lesson in leadership, strategy, and execution. By examining the details, we see that Jesus modeled excellence in execution at every stage—from preparation to organization to distribution and stewardship.

The Setting

The story begins with Jesus withdrawing with His disciples after a busy season of ministry. But instead of finding rest, He encountered a massive crowd of people who followed Him. Matthew notes that He was "moved with compassion" (Matthew

14:14). This emotional foundation is crucial: Jesus' execution of the miracle was rooted in love, not just efficiency. Leaders must remember that true excellence starts with genuine care for people.

The crowd was hungry, tired, and vulnerable. The disciples saw scarcity and suggested sending the people away. Jesus saw opportunity. He replied, "You give them something to eat" (Mark 6:37). This moment reframed the challenge: leadership doesn't dismiss needs—it meets them with faith and strategy.

The Resources

John's Gospel highlights that a boy had five barley loaves and two small fish (John 6:9). From a human perspective, these resources were laughably inadequate. Yet Jesus didn't despise them. He took what was available, blessed it, and multiplied it.

This teaches us that excellence is not about having unlimited resources—it's about maximizing what you have. Many leaders wait for "enough" before executing, but Jesus shows that "not enough" can become more than enough when stewarded properly.

The Organization

One of the most overlooked details of this miracle is Jesus' emphasis on order. Mark 6:39–40 says, "Then Jesus directed them to have all the people sit down in groups on the green grass. So they sat down in groups of hundreds and fifties."

This was no small feat. Five thousand men, plus women and children, likely meant over ten thousand people. Without organization, chaos would have reigned. By grouping them, Jesus created structure for efficient distribution.

Here we see the principle that order precedes multiplication. Excellence in execution requires structure. Leaders who neglect systems and organization will always struggle with scale.

The Blessing

Before distributing, Jesus looked up to heaven, gave thanks, and blessed the food (Matthew 14:19). This step reminds us that excellence is not just about human effort—it's about divine partnership. Jesus acknowledged the Father as the source, modeling gratitude and dependence.

In leadership, blessing what you have—through gratitude, prayer, and vision—unlocks potential. Complaining about resources shrinks capacity; blessing them multiplies it.

The Distribution

Jesus gave the bread and fish to the disciples, and they distributed it to the people. Notice: He did not feed the entire crowd Himself. He empowered His team to share in the work.

This is a masterclass in delegation. By involving the disciples, He multiplied capacity and trained them for future leadership. Excellence in execution requires empowering others, not hoarding responsibility.

The Outcome

The results were astonishing: "They all ate and were satisfied, and the disciples picked up twelve basketfuls of broken pieces that were left over" (Matthew 14:20). Everyone was fed, no one was left out, and there was surplus. The miracle didn't just meet the need—it exceeded it.

The collection of leftovers is especially significant. Jesus didn't allow abundance to produce waste. Excellence includes stewardship. Leaders who execute well not only deliver results but also manage outcomes responsibly.

Lessons From Jesus' Execution

From this miracle, we learn key insights about execution:

1. Compassion Fuels Excellence. Jesus' execution started with compassion for people's needs. Leaders must let love drive their work.
2. Use What You Have. Don't despise small resources—steward them faithfully, and they can multiply.

3. Bring Order to Chaos. Organization makes large-scale impact possible. Structure is not optional; it is essential.
4. Bless Before You Break. Gratitude unlocks abundance. A thankful heart multiplies limited resources.
5. Empower the Team. Delegation expands capacity and trains others for leadership.
6. Steward the Surplus. Excellence is not just about producing results but managing them wisely.

The Disciples' Growth

It's important to note that this miracle wasn't just for the crowd—it was also for the disciples. By participating in the distribution, they saw firsthand the power of faith and stewardship. Each disciple ended up with a basket of leftovers, a tangible reminder that God provides abundantly when we execute with excellence.

This shows us that excellence in execution not only blesses those we serve but also develops those we lead.

Conclusion

The feeding of the five thousand is more than a miracle—it is a model. Jesus demonstrated that excellence in execution involves compassion, organization, empowerment, gratitude, and stewardship. He took limited resources, applied order and blessing, empowered His team, and delivered abundance.

For leaders today, this passage is a reminder that execution matters. Great ideas must be matched with great stewardship. Limited resources are not an excuse for mediocrity—they are an invitation to excellence. When we execute like Jesus, we not only meet needs but multiply impact, leaving a legacy of abundance and trust.

Business Application — Excellence in Execution for Leaders and Organizations Today

In leadership and business, brilliant ideas are plentiful. Conferences, books, and podcasts overflow with vision statements, strategies, and goals. Yet, the gap between dreaming and delivering remains wide. The truth is simple: execution separates those who imagine from those who influence. Leaders who cannot execute with excellence undermine their credibility, erode trust, and waste potential. Leaders who master execution build momentum, loyalty, and long-term success.

The miracle of feeding the five thousand gives us a vivid framework for excellence in execution. Jesus didn't just perform a miracle—He modeled how to meet overwhelming needs with limited resources and still deliver overflow. For modern organizations, this passage translates into actionable strategies that ensure ideas don't just inspire but also impact.

Why Execution Defines Leadership

1. Execution Builds Trust. Customers, employees, and investors trust leaders who deliver consistently. Every successful execution strengthens confidence. Every failure to follow through weakens it.
2. Execution Scales Vision. Vision may start with a leader, but execution multiplies it through systems and people. Without execution, even the best ideas die in obscurity.
3. Execution Creates Legacy. Followers don't remember what leaders intended to do—they remember what leaders actually did.

As Warren Buffett famously noted, "An idiot with a plan can beat a genius without a plan." We could adapt that: A mediocre vision with excellent execution will outperform a brilliant vision with sloppy execution.

Common Barriers to Excellent Execution

1. Lack of Preparation. Leaders underestimate the resources or systems required to deliver.
2. Poor Organization. Chaos consumes energy. Without structure, teams waste time, duplicate efforts, and miss deadlines.
3. Micromanagement. Leaders who refuse to delegate choke growth and create bottlenecks.

4. Complacency. Settling for "good enough" communicates mediocrity and damages reputation.
5. Failure to Measure. Without tracking outcomes, leaders can't improve execution over time.

Jesus avoided every one of these pitfalls in feeding the five thousand. He prepared, organized, delegated, blessed, and stewarded.

Principles of Excellence in Execution

1. Start With Compassion

Execution is not just mechanical—it is relational. Jesus was moved with compassion before acting. In business, execution must serve people. Leaders should ask: "Does this decision improve life for our customers, employees, or community?" Compassion ensures excellence because it refuses to cut corners that harm people.

2. Use What You Have

Excellence isn't about waiting for abundance. It's about stewarding scarcity well. The boy's lunch became the foundation of a miracle. In organizations, this means starting with current resources—skills, technology, networks—and using them fully instead of waiting for perfect conditions.

3. Bring Order to Chaos

Jesus grouped the crowd in fifties and hundreds. Order allowed efficient distribution. Leaders must implement systems and processes that bring clarity and flow. Tools like project management software, clear communication channels, and defined roles create order that makes large-scale execution possible.

4. Bless the Work

Before breaking bread, Jesus gave thanks. Gratitude shifts perspective from lack to abundance. Leaders who "bless" their work—through gratitude, vision casting, and alignment with higher purpose—create cultures of excellence. Employees who feel valued work with greater care.

5. Empower Others

Jesus didn't feed the crowd by Himself—He gave food to His disciples to distribute. Leaders who empower teams multiply capacity. Delegation is not a loss of control; it is a multiplication of influence. Empowerment requires trust, training, and accountability.

6. Steward the Surplus

After everyone was fed, the disciples collected twelve baskets of leftovers. Nothing was wasted. Leaders must manage outcomes responsibly—tracking results, conserving resources, and reinvesting wisely. Excellence includes stewardship after delivery, not just during execution.

Case Studies of Execution in the Marketplace

- Amazon. Jeff Bezos famously prioritized operational excellence. Fast, reliable shipping wasn't glamorous, but it set a new industry standard and built trust.
- Toyota. The Toyota Production System revolutionized manufacturing by focusing on efficiency, quality, and continuous improvement. Excellence in execution became their competitive edge.
- Chick-fil-A. Their customer service model ensures consistent excellence nationwide. Small details—hospitality, cleanliness, consistency—turn a fast-food chain into a cultural phenomenon.

Each of these organizations mirrors the feeding of the five thousand: start with what you have, bring order, empower teams, and deliver abundance.

Action Steps for Leaders

1. Audit Execution. Identify where your organization excels and where it falters. Are deadlines consistently missed? Is quality inconsistent? Are resources wasted?

2. Clarify Standards. Define what excellence looks like for your team. Be specific: timelines, quality checks, customer experience.
3. Build Systems. Create repeatable processes that ensure consistency. Don't rely on memory or improvisation.
4. Invest in Training. Equip your team with skills to execute at a higher level. Excellence grows as people grow.
5. Delegate Wisely. Empower team members with real responsibility and authority. Monitor results without smothering initiative.
6. Evaluate Outcomes. Collect "leftovers" by learning from every project. What worked? What can improve? How can resources be better stewarded?

Avoiding the Mediocrity Trap

In many organizations, the greatest enemy of excellence is the phrase "good enough." Mediocrity satisfies short-term deadlines but destroys long-term trust. Excellence requires leaders to reject shortcuts and continually raise standards. This doesn't mean chasing perfection; it means committing to consistent quality that reflects integrity and care.

Conclusion

Excellence in execution is the bridge between vision and impact. The miracle of feeding the five thousand shows us that even limited resources, when organized, blessed, and distributed with care, can meet massive needs and create overflow.

For leaders today, the call is clear: stop excusing sloppy execution. Start building systems, empowering teams, and stewarding resources with excellence. Execution is not the glamorous side of leadership, but it is the side that builds trust, multiplies influence, and turns dreams into reality.

If you want to lead like Jesus, don't just inspire people with vision—deliver results with excellence. That's how scarcity becomes abundance and how ideas become legacy.

CHAPTER 13

Branding Through Identity: "I Am" Statements of Jesus

The Principle — Why Clear Identity Builds Strong Branding

At the heart of effective branding lies one essential truth: clarity of identity. A brand is not simply a logo, slogan, or color palette. Those are surface elements. True branding is about who you are, what you stand for, and how consistently that identity is communicated. Brands with clear identity inspire trust, loyalty, and advocacy. Brands without it confuse, frustrate, and eventually fade.

Jesus embodied this principle perfectly. Throughout the Gospels, He made a series of bold declarations known as the "I Am" statements: "I am the bread of life" (John 6:35), "I am the light of the world" (John 8:12), "I am the good shepherd"

(John 10:11), "I am the resurrection and the life" (John 11:25), "I am the way, the truth, and the life" (John 14:6), "I am the true vine" (John 15:1). These statements were not vague. They were powerful expressions of His identity and mission, delivered with clarity, confidence, and consistency.

In them, we find a masterclass in branding: Jesus didn't leave people guessing about who He was. He spoke directly, framed His identity in terms people could understand, and reinforced it through His actions. He was not only telling people what He did—He was telling them who He was.

Why Identity Matters in Branding

1. Clarity Creates Connection. People are drawn to leaders and brands who know who they are. Confusion repels. Clarity attracts.
2. Identity Builds Trust. When words and actions align consistently, people know what to expect. That reliability builds loyalty.
3. Differentiation Requires Identity. In crowded markets, your identity sets you apart. Without it, you blend into noise.
4. Identity Guides Action. A clear brand identity doesn't just shape communication—it shapes decisions. Every choice must align with who you say you are.

Just as Jesus' identity statements guided His ministry, a brand's identity guides its culture, customer experience, and future.

The Danger of Vague Identity

Too many organizations fail at branding because they lack clear identity. They try to be everything to everyone, diluting their message until it means nothing. Jesus, by contrast, never diluted His message. He didn't simply say, "I'm a teacher," or "I'm a healer." He declared, "I am the bread of life," a statement that communicated nourishment, sustenance, and eternal value.

Vagueness breeds weakness. Clarity breeds strength.

Identity Is More Than Description

True identity statements go beyond describing what you do—they declare why you exist. "We sell shoes" is description. "We empower people to walk with confidence" is identity. Jesus didn't just say, "I provide food." He said, "I am the bread of life." That's identity, not just activity.

Brands must move from description to declaration. A clear identity tells people not just what you do, but who you are and why it matters.

Consistency of Identity

Jesus didn't just declare His identity once—He repeated and reinforced it across contexts. Whether speaking to crowds, disciples, or critics, He consistently pointed back to who He was. Branding works the same way: repetition and consistency are essential. People may not believe you the first time, but over time, consistent identity builds recognition and trust.

Identity and Confidence

The "I Am" statements were bold. They didn't apologize. They weren't tentative. Jesus declared His identity with authority. For brands, confidence is vital. If you are uncertain about who you are, your audience will be too. Confidence doesn't mean arrogance—it means conviction.

When you know who you are, you don't need to copy others or chase every trend. You stand firm in your unique value.

Identity Shapes Experience

Jesus' identity was not only spoken—it was lived. When He said, "I am the good shepherd," He backed it up by caring for, protecting, and laying down His life for His followers. Branding must operate the same way. If your identity is "customer-first," then every customer interaction must reflect that. If your identity is "innovation," then everything from product design to problem-solving must embody it.

Words without lived experience are hollow. True identity is confirmed in action.

Principle in Practice

For leaders and organizations, applying the principle of branding through identity involves:

1. Clarify Who You Are. Define your core identity in one sentence. Not what you do, but who you are.
2. Declare Boldly. Share that identity consistently and confidently.
3. Live It Out. Back up your words with action. Consistency builds credibility.
4. Differentiate Clearly. Highlight what sets you apart from others.
5. Repeat Relentlessly. Branding requires reinforcement through repetition across platforms and experiences.

Conclusion

The "I Am" statements of Jesus show us that clarity of identity is the foundation of influence. His bold declarations were not marketing tricks—they were authentic expressions of who He was, reinforced by His life. For leaders today, the principle is the same: people cannot follow what they do not understand.

If you want to lead like Jesus, clarify your identity, declare it boldly, and live it consistently. Branding through identity is not about logos or slogans—it is about knowing who you are and communicating it with conviction.

Biblical Insight — Jesus' "I Am" Statements and Their Significance in the Gospels

One of the most striking features of Jesus' ministry was His repeated use of the phrase "I Am" to describe His identity and mission. These declarations, recorded primarily in the Gospel of John, were not random metaphors. They were intentional, layered with meaning, and designed to reveal His true nature to the world. Each statement connected to the everyday experiences of His listeners, but also carried deep theological weight, echoing God's self-revelation in the Old Testament.

For leaders and believers alike, the "I Am" statements offer profound insight into how identity can be articulated with clarity, authority, and relevance. They show us that Jesus did not leave His audience guessing about who He was. He boldly proclaimed His identity in words and then reinforced those words through action.

The Old Testament Echo: "I Am That I Am"

Before examining each statement, it is important to recognize the foundation. In Exodus 3:14, when Moses asked God for His name, God replied: "I Am That I Am." This divine self-identification revealed God as eternal, self-existent, and unchanging.

When Jesus used the phrase "I Am," He was not simply employing poetic language—He was invoking the very name of

God. This was why His statements often provoked such strong reactions from religious leaders. They understood the claim: Jesus was equating Himself with the eternal God of Israel. His identity statements were both revelation and confrontation.

"I Am the Bread of Life" (John 6:35)

After feeding the five thousand, Jesus declared, "I am the bread of life. Whoever comes to me will never go hungry, and whoever believes in me will never be thirsty."

Bread was the staple food of first-century life. To claim to be the bread of life was to declare that He was essential, sustaining, and satisfying in ways nothing else could be. Just as bread nourishes the body, Jesus nourishes the soul.

For the crowd who had just eaten miraculous bread, this was both relevant and radical. He was saying: "Don't just seek temporary satisfaction—seek eternal sustenance in Me."

"I Am the Light of the World" (John 8:12)

In a culture without electricity, light was precious. Darkness meant danger, uncertainty, and vulnerability. By declaring Himself the light of the world, Jesus claimed to bring clarity, direction, and safety to those lost in spiritual darkness.

This statement carried prophetic weight. Isaiah 9:2 had promised, "The people walking in darkness have seen a great light." In identifying Himself as that light, Jesus positioned

Himself as the fulfillment of Israel's hope and the answer to humanity's deepest need.

"I Am the Gate for the Sheep" (John 10:7)

Shepherds in ancient Israel often slept in the doorway of sheepfolds, becoming the literal "gate" that protected sheep from predators. By calling Himself the gate, Jesus was claiming to be the only entry point into safety, rest, and life with God.

This statement also challenged exclusivity. In a world of competing voices and religious systems, Jesus declared that salvation and security could only be found through Him.

"I Am the Good Shepherd" (John 10:11)

Building on the same imagery, Jesus proclaimed, "I am the good shepherd. The good shepherd lays down his life for the sheep." This contrasted Him with "hired hands" who abandoned the flock in danger.

This was not just metaphor—it was mission. Jesus was foreshadowing the cross, where He would lay down His life for humanity. His identity as shepherd emphasized guidance, protection, intimacy, and sacrifice.

"I Am the Resurrection and the Life" (John 11:25)

At the tomb of Lazarus, Jesus declared, "I am the resurrection and the life. The one who believes in me will live, even though they die."

This was more than comfort—it was confrontation with death itself. By raising Lazarus, Jesus demonstrated that His claim was not empty rhetoric. He alone held authority over life and death. For His listeners, this statement was staggering. It revealed Him as the source not only of spiritual life but also of eternal hope.

"I Am the Way, the Truth, and the Life" (John 14:6)

In His farewell discourse, Jesus told His disciples, "I am the way and the truth and the life. No one comes to the Father except through me."

This statement is one of the most exclusive and defining declarations in Scripture. Jesus did not claim to show a way or reveal some truth. He claimed to be the way, the truth, and the life. This was an identity statement that left no room for ambiguity or pluralism. For His followers, it was a call to clarity. For His critics, it was scandalous.

"I Am the True Vine" (John 15:1)

In the Old Testament, Israel was often referred to as a vine, but one that had failed to bear fruit. By calling Himself the true vine, Jesus declared that He was the true source of life, growth, and fruitfulness. His followers, the branches, could only thrive when connected to Him.

This statement emphasized dependence. Apart from Him, His disciples could do nothing. In Him, they could bear much fruit.

The Collective Impact of the "I Am" Statements

Individually, each statement communicated a unique aspect of Jesus' identity. Collectively, they formed a comprehensive picture:

- Bread — Sustenance.
- Light — Guidance.
- Gate — Security.
- Shepherd — Care and sacrifice.
- Resurrection — Victory over death.
- Way, Truth, Life — Exclusivity and clarity.
- Vine — Source of fruitfulness.

Together, these statements created a "brand identity" for Jesus that was clear, memorable, and transformational.

Lessons for Leaders From Jesus' "I Am" Statements

1. Speak With Clarity. Don't leave people guessing about who you are or what you stand for.
2. Use Relatable Language. Jesus used everyday images. Leaders must also communicate identity in terms their audience understands.
3. Repeat and Reinforce. Jesus didn't say "I Am" once—He repeated it across contexts. Branding requires consistency.
4. Align Words With Actions. Jesus lived His identity. Leaders must ensure their brand promise is matched by lived experience.

Conclusion

The "I Am" statements of Jesus were more than metaphors—they were declarations of divine identity. Rooted in God's eternal name, they revealed His nature as sustainer, guide, protector, savior, and life-giver. They were bold, clear, and unforgettable.

For leaders today, these statements offer a model of branding through identity. Just as Jesus communicated who He was with conviction and consistency, we must articulate our identity with clarity and live it out authentically. Identity that is spoken and embodied leaves a legacy that cannot be forgotten.

Business Application — Building Brands Through Clear Identity

In today's competitive world, where countless voices compete for attention, identity is everything. People don't just buy products—they buy meaning. They don't just follow leaders—they follow identities that inspire trust, confidence, and belonging. Strong brands, like strong leaders, succeed not because they have the loudest message but because they have the clearest identity.

Jesus modeled this with His bold "I Am" statements. He didn't present Himself vaguely. He defined who He was with clarity, consistency, and confidence, then demonstrated that identity through His actions. Businesses, organizations, and personal brands can learn from this model to build lasting influence.

Why Identity Is the Core of Branding

1. Clarity Cuts Through Noise. In an age where consumers are bombarded with thousands of messages daily, clarity is power. A strong identity communicates in one sentence what you are about.
2. Identity Creates Trust. People trust brands that are consistent. When your words, visuals, and actions align, trust grows.
3. Identity Differentiates. In crowded industries, identity is often the only thing that sets you apart. Countless companies may sell shoes, but Nike stands

for empowerment and victory. Countless coffee shops exist, but Starbucks sells belonging.

4. Identity Guides Decision-Making. A clear brand identity serves as a filter. Every decision—products, partnerships, marketing—must align with it.

Without identity, brands drift. With identity, brands thrive.

Lessons From Jesus' Identity Statements

Jesus' "I Am" statements provide a masterclass in branding:

- Clarity. He didn't leave people guessing. He told them exactly who He was.
- Relatability. He used everyday metaphors (bread, light, shepherd, vine) that connected with His audience.
- Repetition. He reinforced His identity consistently across different situations.
- Alignment. His words matched His actions. When He said He was the Good Shepherd, He proved it by laying down His life.

For modern brands, these same principles apply. Clarity, relatability, repetition, and alignment build powerful identities.

Building a Strong Brand Identity

1. Define Who You Are. Go beyond products or services. Ask: "What is the deeper identity we represent?" For example, Apple is not just about computers—it's about creativity and thinking differently.
2. Craft Identity Statements. Like Jesus' "I Am" declarations, create short, bold identity phrases. For instance, "We are the trusted guide for first-time homebuyers" or "We are the most personal fitness experience available."
3. Align Actions With Identity. Words mean little without proof. If your identity is "innovation," your products must innovate. If your identity is "service," your culture must serve.
4. Repeat Relentlessly. Identity must be reinforced across every touchpoint—website, social media, customer service, internal culture. Consistency builds recognition.
5. Evolve Without Losing Core. Identity must adapt to changing times without losing its essence. Coca-Cola has evolved for over 100 years but still embodies refreshment and happiness.

Case Studies of Branding Through Identity

- Nike. Their identity is empowerment through athletic achievement. "Just Do It" communicates grit, determination, and victory. Every ad, product, and partnership reinforces this story.

- Tesla. Their identity is innovation and sustainability. Elon Musk doesn't just sell cars—he sells a vision of a renewable future.
- Chick-fil-A. Their identity is service and hospitality. "It's my pleasure" is not a slogan—it's a lived cultural standard.

These brands don't just sell—they embody identity. Their consistency creates loyalty far beyond products.

Personal Branding Through Identity

Branding isn't only for companies. Leaders, entrepreneurs, and professionals also need clear identity. Ask yourself: "What is my 'I Am' statement?"

Examples:

- "I am a leader who builds trust through integrity."
- "I am a realtor who creates smooth, stress-free transactions for families."
- "I am a coach who helps people unlock their potential."

Your personal identity shapes how people perceive and remember you. Without clarity, you blend in. With clarity, you stand out.

Identity in Customer Experience

Identity is not just declared—it is experienced. Customers judge brands not by slogans but by experiences. If your identity is "excellence," then every touchpoint—from website to packaging to customer service—must feel excellent. If your identity is "family," then your culture must make customers feel like family.

Inconsistency between declared identity and lived experience destroys trust. Alignment between them builds loyalty.

Practical Action Steps

1. Write Your Identity Statement. In one sentence, define who you are. Use bold, simple language.
2. Audit Alignment. Examine every area of your business. Do your actions match your identity? If not, fix the gaps.
3. Embed Identity in Culture. Train your team to embody your identity. Customers should feel it in every interaction.
4. Communicate Consistently. Use your identity statement in marketing, conversations, and culture until it becomes second nature.
5. Live It Daily. Identity is not just words—it's behavior. Lead by example.

Avoiding Branding Mistakes

- Vagueness. Don't use bland, generic phrases like "We're the best" or "We provide quality." Be specific.
- Inconsistency. A brand that shifts identity constantly confuses people. Stick to core identity.
- Copying Others. Borrowing another brand's identity makes you a shadow. Find your unique identity.
- Neglecting Culture. Identity is not just external. If your team doesn't believe it, customers won't either.

Conclusion

Jesus' "I Am" statements provide a timeless model of branding through identity. He spoke with clarity, relatability, consistency, and alignment. His declarations were unforgettable because they were bold and true, and His actions proved them.

Modern leaders and businesses can apply the same principle: define who you are, declare it boldly, align your actions with your words, and repeat it consistently. Identity builds trust, differentiates you in the marketplace, and creates loyalty that outlasts trends.

If you want to lead like Jesus, don't just market products—communicate identity. Don't just describe what you do—declare who you are. That is the essence of branding that transforms organizations and leaves a legacy.

CHAPTER 14

Building Loyalty: Discipleship as Customer Retention

The Principle — Why Loyalty Sustains Growth Beyond Acquisition

In business and leadership, it is tempting to focus primarily on acquisition—getting more customers, more followers, more attention. But while acquisition is important, it is only the beginning. Long-term success is not built on how many people you can attract once, but on how many people you can retain consistently. Loyalty sustains growth far beyond acquisition.

The same principle is true in faith and leadership. Jesus did not simply attract large crowds; He invested deeply in disciples who would remain, grow, and carry the mission forward. Crowds came and went. Disciples endured. This is the difference between hype and legacy. Hype fades when excitement dies down. Legacy multiplies because loyalty has been built.

In the business world, the equivalent of discipleship is customer retention. It's the practice of turning one-time buyers into lifelong advocates. While marketing draws people in, loyalty keeps them engaged. Just as Jesus prioritized discipling twelve over entertaining thousands, businesses that prioritize loyalty over constant new acquisition build sustainable impact.

Why Loyalty Matters More Than Acquisition

1. Retention Is More Profitable. Studies consistently show it costs five to seven times more to acquire a new customer than to retain an existing one. Loyal customers also spend more over time.
2. Loyalty Creates Advocates. A satisfied, loyal customer doesn't just keep buying—they tell others. Word-of-mouth from loyal advocates is the most powerful form of marketing.
3. Loyalty Provides Stability. Constantly chasing new customers leads to instability. Loyalty creates predictable revenue and resilience.
4. Loyalty Builds Legacy. Organizations remembered across generations are those that cultivated loyalty. Apple fans, Harley-Davidson riders, and Disney families don't just consume products—they embody identity.

The Pitfalls of Acquisition-Only Leadership

Leaders and businesses who focus only on acquisition eventually burn out. They spend massive resources attracting new people, while neglecting those they already have. The result is churn: people come in through the front door but slip out the back door.

Jesus avoided this trap. He preached to crowds, yes—but He invested most of His time with a small group of disciples. He poured into them, taught them privately, corrected them, encouraged them, and sent them out. His strategy shows us that retention is the multiplier. By focusing on a few loyal followers, He ensured His mission would endure long after the crowds disappeared.

Loyalty as Relationship, Not Transaction

Loyalty cannot be bought with gimmicks or discounts alone. True loyalty is relational, not transactional. People remain loyal when they feel seen, valued, and cared for. Jesus exemplified this in the way He knew His disciples by name, understood their struggles, and guided them personally.

In business, the same principle applies. Customers may come for the product, but they stay for the relationship. When companies treat customers as numbers, loyalty erodes. When they treat them as people, loyalty deepens.

The Stages of Building Loyalty

1. Attraction. People are drawn initially by curiosity, marketing, or a felt need.
2. Engagement. They experience your product, service, or leadership in action.
3. Trust. Consistent excellence convinces them they can depend on you.
4. Commitment. They align emotionally, identifying with your values and mission.
5. Advocacy. They go beyond loyalty to become ambassadors, spreading the message for you.

Jesus led His disciples through these stages. He first attracted them with miracles and teaching, then engaged them through relationship, built trust through consistency, secured commitment through calls to follow Him, and ultimately transformed them into advocates who spread the gospel worldwide.

The Cost of Building Loyalty

Loyalty takes time, effort, and sacrifice. Jesus spent three years walking daily with His disciples. He explained truths repeatedly, endured their doubts, and invested personally. Many leaders and businesses avoid the cost of retention because it seems slower than acquisition. But the payoff of loyalty is exponential.

Building loyalty means:

- Investing in customer experience.
- Listening to feedback and making improvements.
- Going the extra mile when problems arise.
- Prioritizing long-term trust over short-term profit.

The investment may seem costly, but the return is immeasurable.

Loyalty Is Built Through Consistency

Loyalty grows where consistency exists. Jesus was the same with His disciples in private as He was with crowds in public. He consistently lived His values and reinforced His mission. In business, consistency in quality, service, and communication builds confidence. Inconsistency destroys loyalty quickly.

Every touchpoint matters—emails, packaging, conversations, follow-ups. Each moment is an opportunity to reinforce identity and build trust.

Principle in Practice

To practice loyalty as a leader or organization:

1. Prioritize Relationships Over Numbers. Don't just count customers—care for them.
2. Reward Loyalty. Celebrate and thank those who stay with you.

3. Communicate Regularly. Stay in touch, not only when selling.
4. Deliver Consistently. Excellence builds long-term trust.
5. Develop Advocates. Invite your most loyal followers to share stories and spread your message.

Conclusion

The principle of loyalty is clear: retention is more powerful than acquisition. Crowds come and go, but disciples remain. Customers may purchase once, but loyal advocates purchase repeatedly and bring others with them.

If you want to lead like Jesus, shift focus from temporary excitement to lasting loyalty. Invest deeply in people, serve them consistently, and cultivate relationships that endure. Loyalty sustains growth, multiplies influence, and builds legacy.

Biblical Insight — How Jesus Built Loyalty Through Discipleship in the Gospels

When we study the ministry of Jesus, one of the most remarkable aspects is His ability to attract large crowds yet focus His deepest investment on a few. Thousands followed Him for miracles, healings, and teaching. But out of those crowds, He selected twelve disciples and poured into them intentionally. His strategy reveals that building lasting loyalty requires moving beyond surface attraction to deep relational investment.

The Gospels give us countless insights into how Jesus cultivated loyalty through discipleship. By examining His method, we uncover a divine blueprint for developing followers who do not just consume temporarily but commit for a lifetime.

Jesus Called His Disciples Personally

In Matthew 4:18–22, Jesus called Peter, Andrew, James, and John with the simple but powerful words: "Come, follow me." His invitation was personal, direct, and relational. He didn't launch a mass recruitment campaign—He looked individuals in the eye and called them by name.

This personal approach is foundational to loyalty. People remain loyal not to abstract ideas alone but to personal relationships. By investing in individuals, Jesus showed that discipleship begins with personal connection.

Jesus Invested Time in His Disciples

Jesus lived with His disciples day by day. He walked with them, ate with them, traveled with them, and taught them in both public and private settings. Mark 4:34 notes, "He did not say anything to them without using a parable. But when he was alone with his own disciples, he explained everything."

This extra investment gave His disciples greater clarity and deeper trust. While the crowds heard stories, the disciples received explanations. This intimacy built loyalty because it communicated value: "You matter enough for me to give you more."

Jesus Modeled Consistency

The disciples witnessed Jesus in every situation—teaching crowds, confronting Pharisees, healing the sick, praying alone, and enduring pressure. What they saw was consistency. He was the same in private as He was in public.

Consistency builds loyalty because it builds trust. When followers see that a leader's private life aligns with their public message, loyalty deepens. Hypocrisy destroys loyalty; integrity multiplies it.

Jesus Corrected With Care

Loyalty is not built by ignoring faults—it is built by addressing them with love. Peter, for example, often spoke rashly. In Matthew 16:23, when Peter rebuked Jesus about His coming suffering, Jesus corrected him sharply: "Get behind me, Satan!" Yet, despite the correction, Peter remained loyal because he knew Jesus' love and commitment were genuine.

Correction, when delivered with care and truth, strengthens loyalty by refining character and reinforcing trust.

Jesus Empowered His Disciples

In Luke 9:1–2, Jesus gave the twelve authority to drive out demons and cure diseases, sending them to proclaim the kingdom of God. Later, in Luke 10, He sent out seventy-two others.

This empowerment was essential. Loyalty deepens when followers are trusted with responsibility. Jesus didn't just keep His disciples as passive spectators—He gave them opportunities to grow, serve, and lead. Empowerment transforms followers into partners.

Jesus Served His Disciples

In John 13, on the night before His crucifixion, Jesus washed the feet of His disciples. This act of humility shocked them. Peter initially resisted, saying, "You shall never wash my feet." But Jesus replied, "Unless I wash you, you have no part with me."

By serving His disciples in such a personal way, Jesus demonstrated that leadership is not about being above others but about coming beneath them. This radical service built unshakable loyalty. His disciples would never forget it.

Jesus Prayed for His Disciples

In John 17, Jesus prayed specifically for His disciples, asking the Father to protect them, sanctify them, and unify them. His intercession revealed His deep commitment to their future.

Loyalty grows when people know you are invested not just in their present performance but in their long-term well-being. Jesus' prayer showed that He cared for His disciples beyond His earthly ministry.

Jesus Restored Failing Disciples

Perhaps the most powerful example of loyalty comes after Peter denied Jesus three times. Many leaders would have discarded a follower who failed so publicly. But in John 21, the resurrected Jesus restored Peter, asking three times, "Do you love me?" and then recommissioning him: "Feed my sheep."

This act of grace solidified Peter's loyalty forever. Restoration communicates that loyalty is not dependent on perfection but on relationship.

The Result of Jesus' Investment

Because of His intentional discipleship, the twelve (minus Judas, plus Matthias) became the foundation of the early Church. They carried His mission worldwide, enduring persecution and even martyrdom. Their loyalty was unshakable because it had been forged through years of personal investment, empowerment, correction, service, and restoration.

Crowds came and went, but disciples remained. Jesus' method ensured that His mission didn't die when the excitement faded. Loyalty multiplied legacy.

Lessons for Leaders From Jesus' Model

1. Personalize Relationships. Don't treat followers as numbers. Call them by name, listen to their stories, and connect personally.
2. Invest Time. Loyalty requires proximity. Spend time with those you want to retain.
3. Model Integrity. Be consistent in private and public. Hypocrisy destroys trust.
4. Correct With Love. Don't ignore faults—address them in a way that builds, not breaks.
5. Empower With Responsibility. Give followers opportunities to contribute meaningfully.
6. Serve Radically. True leaders serve those they lead, building lasting loyalty.
7. Pray and Care for Long-Term Well-Being. Show investment beyond immediate results.
8. Restore the Fallen. Loyalty grows deepest when grace is extended.

Conclusion

The Gospels show that Jesus built loyalty not through gimmicks or shallow attraction but through deep discipleship. He called personally, invested time, modeled consistency, corrected with care, empowered with responsibility, served sacrificially, prayed faithfully, and restored graciously. The result was disciples who remained loyal through persecution, trials, and even death.

For leaders today, this is a timeless model. Loyalty is not built overnight. It is cultivated through intentional investment in people's growth, dignity, and well-being. If you want followers, attract crowds. But if you want legacy, build loyalty through discipleship.

Business Application — Customer Retention and Loyalty in the Marketplace

In the business world, most leaders are tempted to chase the next big thing: the next marketing campaign, the next customer, the next sale. While acquisition is exciting, retention is where true growth lies. Customer loyalty is the marketplace equivalent of discipleship. Just as Jesus focused His deepest investment on disciples rather than crowds, wise organizations focus not only on attracting customers but on cultivating relationships that turn buyers into lifelong advocates.

Why Retention Outweighs Acquisition

1. Retention Is More Cost-Effective. Research consistently shows that acquiring a new customer costs five to seven times more than keeping an existing one. Retained customers require less convincing, less advertising, and less persuasion.
2. Loyal Customers Spend More. Studies reveal that loyal customers spend more over time. Once trust is built, they are willing to purchase repeatedly and try new products.
3. Loyalty Drives Advocacy. Loyal customers don't just keep buying—they spread the word. Word-of-mouth referrals are the most powerful, trustworthy, and cost-free marketing available.
4. Retention Builds Stability. In uncertain times, loyal customers provide consistent revenue that sustains organizations through downturns.

Just as Jesus built a foundation by investing in a few, businesses build resilience by investing in loyalty.

Why Businesses Fail at Loyalty

1. Obsessed With Acquisition. Leaders pour resources into flashy marketing campaigns while neglecting existing customers.

2. Transactional Mindset. Customers are treated as numbers, not people. Loyalty erodes when relationships feel cold or impersonal.
3. Inconsistent Experience. A great product delivered once but not consistently breaks trust.
4. Failure to Evolve. Neglecting long-term relationships often leads to irrelevance when competitors innovate.

Crowds may be easy to attract, but they are also easy to lose. True retention requires deeper investment.

Lessons From Jesus Applied to Customer Loyalty

1. Call People Personally

Jesus called His disciples by name. Businesses must also personalize engagement. Use customer names, remember preferences, and communicate personally. Automation is helpful, but personalization builds loyalty.

2. Invest Time and Relationship

Jesus lived daily life with His disciples. Similarly, organizations must nurture long-term relationships with customers. This means follow-up emails, loyalty programs, personal check-ins, and ongoing support after the initial sale.

3. Be Consistent

Jesus was the same in public and private. Consistency builds confidence. For businesses, this means maintaining consistent quality, branding, and service across all platforms and touchpoints.

4. Empower Customers

Jesus empowered His disciples to participate in His mission. Businesses can do the same by inviting customers into the story. For example, user-generated content, customer testimonials, and referral programs empower customers to become partners in spreading the message.

5. Serve Sacrificially

Jesus washed His disciples' feet. Businesses must also go beyond expectations, delighting customers with unexpected service and care. Loyalty grows when customers feel valued, not used.

6. Restore Gracefully

Just as Jesus restored Peter after failure, businesses must learn to restore relationships when things go wrong. A bad experience handled with humility and generosity often creates even deeper loyalty.

Practical Strategies for Building Loyalty

1. Develop Loyalty Programs. Reward repeat customers with benefits, discounts, or exclusive experiences.
2. Prioritize Customer Service. Train employees to treat every interaction as an opportunity to build trust.
3. Gather Feedback. Ask customers what they need, then act on it. People remain loyal to organizations that listen.
4. Communicate Regularly. Stay in touch beyond transactions. Provide value through newsletters, updates, and educational content.
5. Celebrate Milestones. Recognize customer anniversaries, birthdays, or milestones with personalized messages or rewards.
6. Empower Advocacy. Create referral programs and share customer success stories. Loyal customers want to spread the word—make it easy for them.

Examples of Loyalty in the Marketplace

- Apple. Their fans line up overnight for new product launches. Apple has built a culture of loyalty by combining innovative products with a strong identity. Customers don't just buy technology—they buy into a story of creativity and excellence.
- Amazon Prime. By offering consistent value through fast shipping, streaming, and exclusive deals,

Amazon created a loyalty ecosystem that makes customers reluctant to leave.

- Starbucks. Their rewards program, consistent experience, and sense of belonging create a "third place" identity. Customers remain loyal not only for coffee but for community.
- Zappos. Known for legendary customer service, Zappos built loyalty by prioritizing care and generosity over short-term profit.

These examples reveal that loyalty is cultivated intentionally, not by accident.

Turning Customers Into Advocates

Loyalty at its highest level creates advocates. These are people who don't just stay—they bring others. Jesus' disciples became advocates, spreading His message worldwide. Businesses can do the same by empowering loyal customers to tell their stories, share reviews, and invite others into the brand experience.

When customers become storytellers, loyalty moves from retention to multiplication.

The Cost and Reward of Loyalty

Building loyalty requires patience, sacrifice, and intentionality. It may mean longer follow-up processes, higher investments in service, and slower but steadier growth. Yet the reward is exponential. Loyalty reduces marketing costs, stabilizes revenue, and creates advocates who grow the brand for free.

As Jesus demonstrated, legacy is not built by temporary crowds but by loyal disciples. The same is true in the marketplace: legacy brands are those that cultivated loyalty intentionally and consistently.

Conclusion

Customer loyalty is the foundation of sustainable growth. Like discipleship in the Gospels, loyalty requires personal connection, consistency, empowerment, service, and restoration. It cannot be faked or forced—it must be cultivated intentionally.

If you want to lead like Jesus, don't just chase crowds or quick sales. Invest in loyalty. Care for customers, serve them well, and empower them to become advocates. Loyalty transforms customers into partners, transactions into relationships, and businesses into legacies.

CHAPTER 15

Legacy and Succession: The Great Commission

The Principle — Why Legacy and Succession Secure the Future of Leadership

Every great leader eventually faces the same question: What happens after me? Vision, strategy, and influence are powerful, but if they end with the leader, their impact is temporary. True leadership is measured not only by what you build in your lifetime but by what continues after you are gone. Legacy and succession are the ultimate tests of leadership.

Jesus modeled this principle perfectly. His earthly ministry lasted just over three years, yet His mission continues across millennia because He planned for legacy and succession. He did not aim to keep crowds dependent on His physical presence. Instead, He prepared disciples to carry His mission forward. Before His ascension, He gave them the Great Commission: "Therefore go and make disciples of all nations, baptizing them in the name of the Father and of the Son and of the Holy Spirit, and teaching them to obey everything I have commanded you. And surely I am with you always, to the very end of the age" (Matthew 28:19–20).

This commission was more than instruction—it was succession planning. Jesus ensured His mission would outlive Him by empowering successors who would multiply disciples and spread the gospel worldwide.

Why Legacy Matters

1. Vision Without Legacy Dies. If a leader does not prepare for succession, the vision collapses when they step aside.
2. Legacy Multiplies Impact. A leader's influence expands exponentially when successors carry the mission further.
3. Legacy Brings Meaning. Leadership is not just about success in the moment but about significance that endures across generations.

True leadership asks: "How will what I've built continue without me?"

Why Succession Is Essential

Succession ensures continuity. Without it, even great movements collapse. Consider how businesses or organizations often decline after the founder departs because no plan for succession exists. Jesus avoided this mistake. He trained disciples, invested in them, empowered them, and then entrusted them with the mission.

Succession requires intentionality:

- Selecting Successors. Jesus chose twelve, not hundreds.
- Training Successors. He walked with them daily, teaching and correcting.
- Empowering Successors. He gave them authority to heal, preach, and lead before His departure.
- Commissioning Successors. He sent them out with clear instructions and confidence in their calling.

Leaders who fail at succession often do so because of insecurity, pride, or shortsightedness. But leaders who succeed ensure their mission multiplies.

The Dangers of Neglecting Legacy and Succession

1. Collapse of the Mission. Without succession, vision dies with the leader.
2. Confusion and Division. Lack of clarity about who leads next creates chaos.
3. Wasted Investment. Years of effort are squandered if no one carries it forward.

History is filled with organizations, movements, and even nations that crumbled because leaders failed to prepare successors.

Legacy Is Built Through People

Buildings crumble. Strategies shift. Markets change. The only true carriers of legacy are people. Jesus didn't leave behind books He wrote or monuments He built. He left behind disciples. His investment in people ensured that His message could spread across time and culture.

Leaders today must remember: your true legacy is not your projects or profits but the people you equip, empower, and inspire.

Succession Requires Letting Go

One of the hardest parts of succession is letting go of control. Many leaders cling tightly to power, unwilling to trust others with responsibility. Jesus, however, let go. He told His disciples, "Very truly I tell you, whoever believes in me will do the works I have been doing, and they will do even greater things than these" (John 14:12).

He not only released them to continue His work but also promised they would surpass Him in reach. That level of humility and empowerment is the essence of great succession.

Legacy vs. Popularity

Crowds followed Jesus for miracles, but His true legacy was not the thousands who came and went. It was the disciples who stayed, grew, and carried the mission. Popularity fades, but legacy remains. Leaders must resist the temptation to focus only on popularity metrics—followers, sales, attention—and instead invest in legacy, which comes from developing others.

Principle in Practice

To apply the principle of legacy and succession, leaders must:

1. Think Beyond Yourself. Define your vision in terms of what will outlive you.
2. Identify Successors Early. Begin investing in people before you need them.
3. Transfer Knowledge. Share wisdom, experiences, and values consistently.
4. Empower Before You Exit. Give successors real responsibility while you are still present to guide them.
5. Release With Confidence. Trust successors to carry the mission forward, even if they lead differently.

Conclusion

Legacy and succession are the ultimate measures of leadership. Jesus' Great Commission was not just a command—it was a succession plan that ensured His mission would continue through disciples across generations. He invested in people, empowered them, and released them with confidence.

For leaders today, the call is the same: don't let your vision die with you. Build legacy by investing in people. Secure succession by empowering others to carry the mission forward. True leadership is not proven in what happens while you lead but in what continues after you are gone.

Biblical Insight — The Great Commission as Jesus' Succession Plan in the Gospels

When Jesus rose from the dead and prepared to ascend to the Father, He left His disciples with final words that have echoed across centuries: the Great Commission. Found in Matthew 28:18–20, Mark 16:15–18, Luke 24:46–49, John 20:21–23, and Acts 1:8, this commission was not merely a farewell—it was a carefully designed succession plan. Jesus was handing over leadership of the mission to His disciples, entrusting them to continue and multiply the work He had begun.

The Great Commission reveals how Jesus prepared His followers to transition from dependence on His physical presence to reliance on His Spirit and leadership. It shows us that true legacy is not built on crowds, monuments, or temporary popularity but on empowering successors who carry the mission forward.

The Authority Behind the Commission

In Matthew 28:18, Jesus begins His commission by declaring, "All authority in heaven and on earth has been given to me." This statement is crucial. Before delegating responsibility, Jesus established His authority.

He was not sending the disciples out on their own power. He was delegating His authority to them. Succession requires clarity of authority—leaders must establish the foundation from which their successors will lead. Without authority, successors lack confidence and legitimacy. By grounding the mission in His authority, Jesus gave His disciples both confidence and security.

The Clarity of the Mission

Jesus gave clear instructions: "Go and make disciples of all nations, baptizing them … and teaching them to obey everything I have commanded you" (Matthew 28:19–20).

The mission was not vague. It was specific:

- Go. Take initiative, don't wait.
- Make disciples. Multiply, don't just gather.
- Of all nations. Expand globally, not just locally.
- Baptize. Establish identity and belonging.
- Teach obedience. Develop maturity, not just knowledge.

Succession requires clarity. Ambiguity breeds confusion. Jesus made the mission unmistakable, ensuring His disciples knew exactly what they were to do.

The Empowerment of the Spirit

In Acts 1:8, Jesus told His disciples, "But you will receive power when the Holy Spirit comes on you; and you will be my witnesses in Jerusalem, and in all Judea and Samaria, and to the ends of the earth."

This empowerment was essential. Jesus did not expect His disciples to fulfill the mission in their own strength. He promised the Holy Spirit as the power source.

Succession requires not only delegation but empowerment. Without empowerment, successors may have responsibility but lack capacity. Jesus bridged that gap by promising divine empowerment that would fuel their success.

The Strategy of Multiplication

The Great Commission emphasized discipleship, not just conversion. Jesus didn't instruct His followers to gather crowds or count decisions. He told them to make disciples—to invest deeply in others who would then go and make more disciples.

This is the principle of multiplication. One disciple makes another, who makes another, creating exponential growth. Succession is never about addition—it is about multiplication.

Jesus' model ensured that the gospel would spread across cultures and generations through intentional reproduction.

The Promise of His Presence

Jesus concluded the Great Commission with a promise: "And surely I am with you always, to the very end of the age" (Matthew 28:20). Though He would no longer be physically present, His presence would remain spiritually through the Holy Spirit.

Succession can often feel like abandonment. But Jesus reassured His disciples that they were not alone. Leaders who successfully transition must also offer presence—mentorship, encouragement, and assurance—that empowers successors to move forward with confidence.

The Immediate Response of the Disciples

The book of Acts shows how the disciples embraced the succession plan. They waited for the Spirit in obedience (Acts 1:12–14), received power at Pentecost (Acts 2), and immediately began preaching, baptizing, and making disciples. By Acts 4, thousands had joined the movement.

This rapid expansion was not the result of new strategy—it was the fruit of succession. Jesus had prepared them, and they executed His mission with power.

Biblical Examples of Succession Echoed

The Great Commission mirrors earlier biblical patterns of succession.

- Moses prepared Joshua to lead Israel into the Promised Land (Deuteronomy 31:7–8).
- Elijah passed his mantle to Elisha (2 Kings 2:9–14).
- David prepared Solomon to build the temple (1 Chronicles 28).

In each case, succession involved preparation, empowerment, and commissioning. Jesus fulfilled and surpassed this pattern, commissioning His disciples not just for one nation but for all nations.

Lessons From Jesus' Succession Plan

1. Establish Authority. Ensure successors know they lead from delegated authority, not personal ambition.
2. Give Clear Mission. Succession requires clarity of goals and responsibilities.
3. Empower With Resources. Delegation without empowerment sets successors up to fail.
4. Build Multiplication, Not Dependence. Invest in people who will reproduce, not just consume.
5. Offer Continued Presence. Provide encouragement and assurance during transition.

Conclusion

The Great Commission was Jesus' succession plan. It transferred responsibility, clarified mission, delegated authority, promised empowerment, and ensured presence. The result was a movement that spread from a small band of disciples in Jerusalem to every corner of the globe.

For leaders today, this biblical insight is profound: succession is not an afterthought—it is the capstone of leadership. Legacy is not built by what you do during your lifetime but by how well you prepare others to carry the mission forward.

Jesus shows us that the best succession plans are marked by clarity, empowerment, multiplication, and assurance. Leaders who follow His example secure a legacy that endures beyond themselves.

Business Application — Legacy and Succession Planning in Organizations Today

In the world of leadership, organizations rise and fall not only because of vision but also because of succession. Many companies, ministries, and even nations crumble when the founding leader departs because there was no plan for continuity. Ideas may be strong, strategies may be effective, but without succession, the mission dies with the leader.

Jesus' model in the Great Commission offers timeless wisdom for how modern leaders can prepare for legacy. He understood that the true test of leadership is not what happens while you are present, but what continues after you are gone. The same principle applies in business: your leadership is only as strong as its ability to endure beyond you.

Why Succession Planning Matters in Business

1. Continuity of Vision. Without succession, organizations lose momentum and direction when leadership changes.
2. Retention of Talent. Clear succession paths inspire loyalty among employees who see opportunities to grow.
3. Trust of Stakeholders. Investors, customers, and partners gain confidence when they know an organization has stability beyond one leader.
4. Sustainability of Mission. Succession ensures the mission remains intact even when circumstances or leadership change.

Succession is not optional—it is essential. Leaders who avoid it because of fear or pride endanger the very organizations they have built.

Why Many Leaders Fail at Succession

1. Ego and Insecurity. Some leaders want to be irreplaceable. Their pride blinds them from preparing others.
2. Short-Term Thinking. Leaders focus on immediate results without considering long-term continuity.
3. Fear of Change. Preparing successors requires letting go, which many leaders resist.
4. Neglect of People. Leaders who prioritize projects over people often fail to develop successors capable of carrying the mission.

Failure to plan succession is not just an oversight—it is leadership negligence.

Lessons From Jesus for Succession Planning

1. Establish Authority Clearly

Just as Jesus declared, "All authority in heaven and on earth has been given to me" (Matthew 28:18), leaders must clarify the source of authority and delegate it intentionally. Successors must know they are leading with legitimacy, not as placeholders.

2. Clarify the Mission

Jesus gave clear instructions: "Go and make disciples of all nations." Succession requires mission clarity. Successors cannot continue a vision that is vague or unarticulated. Leaders must define core values, goals, and non-negotiables.

3. Empower With Resources

Jesus promised the Holy Spirit's empowerment (Acts 1:8). Likewise, leaders must ensure successors are resourced with training, finances, and authority to succeed. Delegation without empowerment is setting successors up for failure.

4. Focus on Multiplication

Jesus emphasized discipleship that multiplies. In organizations, succession must prepare leaders who can develop other leaders. Multiplication, not dependence, ensures lasting impact.

5. Provide Continued Presence and Support

Jesus reassured His disciples, "I am with you always." Modern leaders can provide presence through mentorship, advisory roles, or transitional support. This continuity offers confidence during change.

Practical Strategies for Succession in Business

1. Identify Potential Successors Early. Spot talent in your organization who embody values and vision. Don't wait until retirement to think about who will lead next.
2. Invest in Leadership Development. Provide training, mentorship, and growth opportunities. Create a leadership pipeline rather than waiting for replacements to appear.
3. Delegate Responsibility Gradually. Give potential successors real opportunities to lead, fail, and learn while you are still present to guide.
4. Document Vision and Systems. Ensure your mission, processes, and culture are clearly articulated in writing. Oral tradition alone is fragile.
5. Communicate Succession Transparently. Let stakeholders know that succession is part of the plan. Transparency builds trust and prevents confusion.
6. Release With Confidence. Eventually, leaders must step back. Trust successors, even if they lead differently. Succession is not about cloning yourself—it's about continuing the mission.

Case Studies in Succession

- Apple. When Steve Jobs prepared to step aside, he positioned Tim Cook as his successor. Though Cook led differently, Apple continued to thrive because succession was intentional.

- Disney. The company has faced both success and failure in succession, demonstrating the importance of careful planning and cultural alignment.
- Chick-fil-A. Founder Truett Cathy built succession into the company's DNA by preparing family and leaders who carried forward both the business and the values.
- Kodak. In contrast, Kodak failed to prepare for leadership and industry succession, clinging to outdated strategies. The result was decline despite once being dominant.

Succession determines whether organizations adapt and thrive or fade into irrelevance.

Building Legacy Beyond Succession

Succession is about leadership continuity, but legacy is about significance. Legacy ensures that the values, culture, and mission endure beyond both the leader and even the successors. Jesus' legacy was not just the disciples who followed Him but the values of the Kingdom that continue to shape lives centuries later.

Leaders must therefore ask: "What values do I want to outlive me?" Projects may end, markets may change, but values create culture. Legacy is the culture that carries vision forward.

Action Steps for Leaders

1. Write Your Legacy Statement. Define what you want to be remembered for.
2. Develop a Succession Plan. Outline how leadership will transition and who is being prepared.
3. Build a Leadership Pipeline. Create layers of leaders, not just one successor.
4. Live Legacy Now. Model values daily so they become embedded in culture.
5. Release With Joy. See succession not as loss but as multiplication.

Conclusion

Legacy and succession are not optional—they are the pinnacle of leadership responsibility. Jesus modeled succession through the Great Commission, establishing authority, clarifying mission, empowering with resources, promising presence, and focusing on multiplication. The result was a movement that outlived Him and continues today.

Modern organizations must embrace the same principle. Don't let your mission collapse because you failed to prepare successors. Invest in people, clarify identity, empower with resources, and release with confidence. Legacy is not proven by what you build in your lifetime but by what endures beyond it.

If you want to lead like Jesus, don't just build success—build succession. Don't just live for popularity—live for legacy. That is leadership that multiplies impact for generations.

CHAPTER 16

Conclusion: Leading Like Jesus in the Marketplace

The Principle — Why Leading Like Jesus Transforms Both Life and Business

Every book has a destination, and every journey has a climax. The journey we've taken through the principles, practices, and strategies of Jesus' life and ministry now comes to a conclusion. From His clarity of identity, to His strategic timing, to His storytelling, to His excellence in execution, to His focus on loyalty, and finally to His preparation for legacy, Jesus displayed the most complete model of leadership the world has ever seen.

The principle that ties everything together is this: Leading like Jesus is not about copying tactics—it's about embodying His values.

Too often in the marketplace, leadership is reduced to formulas and shortcuts. Bookshelves overflow with "10 steps to success" or "5 hacks to influence." While these tools have their place, they cannot replace character. Leadership that lasts is not built on manipulation or hype; it is built on values that shape people, inspire trust, and leave a legacy. Jesus' leadership was values-driven. That is why it remains timeless.

The Core Values of Leading Like Jesus

1. Identity Rooted in Purpose

Jesus never wavered in His identity. He declared boldly who He was: the bread of life, the light of the world, the good shepherd. For leaders today, identity is the foundation of influence. Without clarity of purpose and authenticity of identity, branding collapses, teams scatter, and customers lose trust.

2. Strategic Timing

Jesus never rushed, never lagged, and never missed His moment. He knew when to wait and when to act. Leaders must learn to balance patience with boldness. Success often hinges not only on the idea but on the timing of its execution.

3. The Power of Story

Jesus wrapped eternal truths in relatable parables that stuck for generations. Leaders who master storytelling create emotional connection, drive loyalty, and multiply influence. In an age of endless information, stories are what people remember.

4. Excellence in Execution

Jesus turned five loaves and two fish into abundance through order, blessing, and distribution. Leaders must understand that vision without execution frustrates, but execution with excellence multiplies. Details matter. Stewardship matters. Consistency matters.

5. Building Loyalty Through Relationship

Jesus focused on discipleship, not crowds. Crowds came and went, but disciples stayed, grew, and carried the mission forward. Businesses too must prioritize customer retention, relational depth, and long-term loyalty over short-term hype.

6. Legacy and Succession

Jesus' Great Commission was the ultimate succession plan. He invested in people who would multiply the mission. Leaders must prepare successors, develop pipelines of talent, and focus on values that outlast their own leadership.

These six values, drawn from Jesus' example, are the framework of leading with integrity, impact, and endurance.

Why This Principle Matters for the Marketplace

The marketplace is filled with competition, pressure, and constant change. Leaders face the temptation to compromise values for quick wins, to prioritize growth over integrity, and to chase popularity rather than build legacy. But leading like Jesus provides an alternative:

1. Clarity in Chaos. In a noisy, uncertain world, values rooted in Jesus provide unshakable clarity.
2. Trust in Transactions. Trust is the ultimate currency of business. Leading like Jesus builds trust by aligning words with actions.
3. Human Connection. Business is not just about products—it's about people. Jesus prioritized people above programs.
4. Enduring Impact. Trends come and go, but values leave legacies. Organizations that lead like Jesus don't just succeed—they endure.

The Marketplace as a Mission Field

Jesus often used the language of work—farming, fishing, shepherding, trading—to illustrate His teaching. He understood that the marketplace is not separate from faith but a central arena for it. Leaders today must see their businesses not only as places for profit but as platforms for impact.

When you lead like Jesus in the marketplace, you transform transactions into testimonies. Customers experience not just a service but a relationship. Employees experience not just a paycheck but purpose. Communities experience not just economic growth but cultural renewal.

The Principle in Practice

To lead like Jesus in the marketplace, leaders must commit to three ongoing disciplines:

1. Embodiment. Don't just preach values—live them. Let your integrity, humility, and consistency embody the message.
2. Investment. Pour into people, not just projects. Your greatest asset is not your product but your people.
3. Multiplication. Train others to lead with the same values. Don't aim to be irreplaceable—aim to be reproducible.

This is how legacy is built.

Conclusion

The principle of leading like Jesus is not about religious jargon or abstract spirituality—it is about practical, timeless leadership values that transform both people and organizations. His model proves that the most effective leadership is servant leadership, the most powerful branding is identity-driven, the most sustainable growth comes from loyalty, and the most enduring impact comes from legacy.

If you want to lead like Jesus, embrace these values. Live them in your home, your community, and your business. Let your leadership reflect His clarity, timing, storytelling, excellence, loyalty, and legacy.

Leadership is not just about the bottom line. It is about the people you impact, the culture you create, and the legacy you leave. Jesus showed us the way. Now it's our turn to follow.

Biblical Insight — Jesus' Leadership as the Model for All Generations in the Gospels

When we survey the Gospels—Matthew, Mark, Luke, and John—we see more than miracles, parables, or theological discourses. We see a living model of leadership. Jesus was not simply a spiritual teacher; He was the greatest leader who ever walked the earth. His leadership has shaped history, outlasted empires, and transformed billions of lives. Unlike human leaders whose influence fades with time, Jesus' leadership endures because it was rooted in eternal truth and timeless values.

This section explores the biblical insight that Jesus' leadership is not locked in the first century—it is relevant for every generation. His principles apply in homes, churches, communities, and marketplaces today. Whether leading a family, a business, or a nation, the Gospels reveal His leadership as the ultimate model.

Jesus Led With Identity

From the beginning of His ministry, Jesus was clear about who He was. At His baptism, the Father declared: "This is my beloved Son, in whom I am well pleased" (Matthew 3:17). This affirmation grounded His identity before He preached a sermon, performed a miracle, or called a disciple.

Throughout the Gospels, Jesus reinforced this identity through His "I Am" statements. He knew who He was and declared it boldly. Unlike many leaders who seek affirmation from others, Jesus led from the security of His identity in the Father.

For every generation, this is a foundational insight: leadership must begin with identity. Insecure leaders create insecure cultures. Confident leaders, rooted in God's affirmation, create stability and trust.

Jesus Led With Vision

Jesus consistently cast vision for the Kingdom of God. He declared, "Repent, for the kingdom of heaven has come near" (Matthew 4:17). His parables illustrated what the Kingdom was like—mustard seeds, hidden treasure, a pearl of great price. He painted pictures of a better reality that stirred imagination and inspired commitment.

Visionary leadership is timeless. Leaders in every era must offer people more than tasks—they must offer a picture of a future worth pursuing. Jesus shows us that vision must be clear, compelling, and connected to values.

Jesus Led With Timing

The Gospels highlight Jesus' sensitivity to timing. At the wedding in Cana, He said, "My hour has not yet come" (John 2:4). When crowds tried to seize Him, the writers note, "His hour had not yet come" (John 7:30). But when the cross approached, He declared, "The hour has come" (John 12:23).

This shows us that leadership requires discernment of timing. Acting too soon or too late can derail a mission. Jesus modeled perfect timing, demonstrating patience when necessary and boldness when the moment was right. For leaders in every generation, discernment of timing is essential.

Jesus Led With Story

No leader in history has used story as effectively as Jesus. The Gospels overflow with parables—the sower, the prodigal son, the Good Samaritan. These stories were simple, memorable, and deeply profound. They explained complex truths in language ordinary people understood.

Storytelling remains one of the most powerful tools of leadership. Whether teaching children, inspiring employees, or casting vision for a movement, leaders who use story connect at the level of the heart. Jesus' example proves that truth wrapped in narrative has the power to endure across cultures and centuries.

Jesus Led With Excellence in Execution

Jesus didn't just teach—He delivered. When five thousand men plus women and children were hungry, He didn't panic. He organized, blessed, multiplied, and distributed food until everyone was satisfied, with twelve baskets left over (Matthew 14:13–21). His execution was marked by order, empowerment, and stewardship.

This shows us that leadership is not measured only by ideas but by execution. Every generation needs leaders who can deliver consistently, steward resources wisely, and build systems that multiply impact.

Jesus Led With Relationship and Loyalty

The Gospels reveal that while Jesus preached to multitudes, His deepest investment was in a small group of disciples. He called them personally, lived with them daily, corrected them, empowered them, and even washed their feet (John 13). His loyalty to them built their loyalty to Him.

True leadership is relational. Crowds come and go, but loyal followers remain. Every generation needs leaders who invest in people, not just numbers. Jesus' discipleship model shows us that relationships build retention, and retention builds legacy.

Jesus Led With Succession in Mind

Finally, Jesus prepared for legacy. He didn't keep His disciples dependent on His physical presence. Instead, He commissioned them: "Go and make disciples of all nations" (Matthew 28:19). He promised the Spirit's empowerment and sent them to multiply.

Succession is the mark of enduring leadership. Jesus' preparation ensured that His mission continued beyond His lifetime. For leaders in any age, succession is non-negotiable. Without it, even great movements collapse.

Jesus' Leadership Compared to Human Models

The Gospels contrast Jesus' leadership with the rulers of His day. In Matthew 20:25–26, He told His disciples: "The rulers of the Gentiles lord it over them … Not so with you. Instead, whoever wants to become great among you must be your servant."

Where human leaders pursued dominance, Jesus modeled service. Where others sought power, He demonstrated humility. Where others built empires, He built people. This servant-leadership model is timeless. It works in families, churches, communities, and corporations because it aligns with the deepest needs of the human heart.

Lessons for All Generations

From the Gospels, we can distill timeless insights for leadership:

1. Identity anchors leadership. Know who you are before leading others.
2. Vision inspires commitment. Paint a picture of a better future.
3. Timing determines success. Act with discernment and patience.
4. Story connects deeply. Use narrative to make truth memorable.
5. Execution builds trust. Deliver consistently with excellence.
6. Relationships create loyalty. Invest in people, not just numbers.
7. Succession secures legacy. Prepare others to continue the mission.

Conclusion

The Gospels present Jesus not only as Savior but also as the ultimate leader. His identity, vision, timing, storytelling, execution, relational depth, and succession planning created a leadership model that has endured for over two thousand years. His influence has shaped individuals, communities, and civilizations, proving that His way of leading is not bound by time or culture.

For every generation, including ours, Jesus' leadership remains the standard. Leaders who embrace His model will not only achieve success but will create significance. They will not only build organizations but will build legacies.

The insight is clear: leadership modeled after Jesus is leadership that lasts.

Business Application — Applying Jesus' Leadership Model to Modern Organizations and the Marketplace

Leadership in today's marketplace is under more pressure than ever. Technology evolves rapidly, competition is fierce, and trust in institutions is at historic lows. Customers, employees, and communities are not just looking for leaders who can make money—they're looking for leaders they can trust, follow, and believe in. This is where Jesus' leadership model, revealed in the Gospels, speaks with stunning relevance. His leadership was timeless because it was not built on charisma alone but on character, clarity, and conviction.

The question for modern leaders is simple: How do we apply Jesus' model of leadership in organizations and the marketplace today?

Identity-Driven Branding and Leadership

Jesus began with identity: "I am the bread of life … the light of the world … the good shepherd." In the marketplace, clarity of identity is just as vital. Companies that thrive know exactly who they are and communicate it consistently.

- Apple stands for creativity and innovation.
- Nike embodies empowerment and achievement.
- Patagonia represents sustainability and responsibility.

Each of these brands demonstrates clarity of identity. Leaders must ask: What is our "I Am" statement? Identity-driven leadership builds trust, attracts loyalty, and creates clarity in decision-making.

Strategic Timing in Decision-Making

Jesus showed perfect awareness of timing—refusing to be rushed at Cana and declaring "My hour has come" when it was time for the cross. Businesses must also develop discernment about timing. Launching too early can kill a product. Waiting too long can let competitors dominate.

Practical application:

- Conduct timing reviews before major launches.
- Build flexibility into strategies to adjust when conditions shift.

- Recognize that sometimes waiting is as strategic as acting.

Strategic timing is not guesswork—it is the discipline of discernment.

Storytelling as a Marketplace Advantage

Jesus taught in parables because stories move people more than facts. Modern businesses must recover the art of storytelling. Data informs, but stories inspire.

- Airbnb tells the story of belonging anywhere in the world.
- TOMS Shoes built a movement by telling stories of shoes given to children in need.
- Charity: Water shares stories of lives transformed by clean water.

For leaders, storytelling should not just describe what you sell but why it matters. A clear story turns customers into advocates.

Excellence in Execution

The feeding of the five thousand teaches us that order, stewardship, and empowerment create abundance. In organizations today, excellence in execution is often what separates great companies from mediocre ones.

Practical applications include:

- Building systems that scale without chaos.
- Training teams to focus on quality at every level.
- Treating resources with respect to avoid waste.

Excellence builds reputation. Mediocrity erodes it. Leaders who prioritize excellence deliver impact that lasts.

Building Loyalty Through Relationships

Jesus built loyalty by discipling twelve rather than entertaining thousands. Businesses must embrace this principle by prioritizing customer retention over constant acquisition. Loyal customers spend more, stay longer, and bring others with them.

Practical applications:

- Develop loyalty programs that reward repeat customers.
- Personalize experiences so customers feel seen and valued.
- Follow up after the sale to turn transactions into relationships.

The goal is not just customers but advocates—people who carry your message voluntarily.

Succession and Legacy in Organizations

The Great Commission shows that succession was always part of Jesus' plan. In organizations, succession planning is often neglected until it's too late. Leaders must think about who will lead after them and prepare successors with clarity and empowerment.

Practical steps include:

- Identifying potential leaders early.
- Creating leadership development pipelines.
- Delegating real responsibility before transition.
- Embedding values into culture so they outlast any one leader.

Organizations that plan succession well (like Chick-fil-A or Apple) thrive for decades. Those that neglect it (like Kodak or Blockbuster) collapse.

Servant Leadership as Cultural Advantage

Jesus redefined greatness: "Whoever wants to become great among you must be your servant" (Matthew 20:26). Modern workplaces are shifting toward the same principle. Employees today don't want dictators—they want servant-leaders who empower, listen, and build cultures of trust.

Practical appli cations:

- Leaders modeling humility rather than dominance.
- Organizations prioritizing employee development over exploitation.
- Cultures where leaders serve first, creating environments where teams thrive.

Servant leadership builds loyalty internally, which translates to loyalty externally.

Integrating Jesus' Model Into Daily Leadership

To apply Jesus' leadership model practically in the marketplace, leaders can commit to these rhythms:

1. Identity Check. Begin every quarter with a review of core identity. Ask: Are we still who we say we are?
2. Timing Discernment. Before launches or pivots, pause to discern if conditions align.
3. Storytelling Practice. Regularly collect and share stories of impact within your team and with customers.
4. Execution Review. Evaluate projects not just for completion but for excellence.
5. Loyalty Metrics. Track retention, not just acquisition. Ask: How well are we serving those already with us?

6. Succession Planning. Dedicate time annually to identify and develop emerging leaders.

These practices ensure that leadership is not reactive but intentional.

Avoiding Pitfalls

Leaders often fail because they:

- Drift from identity.
- Rush or delay timing.
- Overload on data while neglecting story.
- Execute sloppily.
- Chase new customers while ignoring existing ones.
- Avoid planning succession out of fear or pride.

By studying Jesus' model, leaders gain a framework that prevents these pitfalls.

Conclusion

Jesus' leadership is not confined to religious contexts—it is the blueprint for enduring success in every sphere, including the marketplace. His clarity of identity, strategic timing, storytelling, excellence in execution, relational loyalty, and focus on succession provide a comprehensive framework for leadership today.

Modern leaders who embrace this model will build organizations that not only succeed but endure. They will create cultures of trust, teams of loyalty, and legacies of impact. They will prove that the marketplace can be more than a place for profit—it can be a platform for purpose.

If you want to lead like Jesus in the marketplace, embody His values, apply His methods, and pursue His legacy. Success may fade, but significance endures. The model of Jesus ensures that your leadership, like His, will outlast you and transform the world.

EPILOGUE

The Call to Lead Like Jesus

Leadership is not easy. The pressures of the marketplace, the weight of responsibility, and the lure of compromise can wear even the strongest leaders down. Yet, the model of Jesus stands as both an invitation and a challenge. He shows us that leadership is not about self-promotion but service, not about control but empowerment, not about popularity but legacy.

We have walked through His principles:

- Identity that is bold and clear.
- Timing that discerns seasons with wisdom.
- Storytelling that moves hearts.
- Excellence in execution that multiplies impact.
- Loyalty through relationships that endures beyond the crowd.
- Succession that secures legacy for generations.

These are not just strategies for business—they are truths for life. Whether you are leading a company, a community, a congregation, or a family, the leadership of Jesus offers a blueprint that transcends time and culture.

The ultimate question is not whether you will lead, but how you will lead. Will you lead for applause, or will you lead for legacy? Will you lead for profit alone, or for purpose that outlasts you? Will you lead like the rulers of the world who "lord it over" others, or will you lead like Jesus who stooped to wash His disciples' feet?

The world is desperate for leaders of integrity. Employees long for leaders who see them as people, not numbers. Customers long for companies that value more than transactions. Communities long for organizations that give back rather than only take. Families long for examples of faithfulness and love.

You are called to be that kind of leader.

To lead like Jesus is to embrace values that are countercultural yet timeless. It is to live with conviction, serve with humility, and lead with clarity. It is to understand that leadership is not about what you accomplish during your lifetime but about what continues because of how you lived.

As you step forward, take courage. You may not have all the resources, influence, or answers—but you have the ultimate model. Jesus Christ, the greatest leader who ever lived, calls you to follow in His footsteps. His Spirit empowers you. His example guides you. His legacy invites you to add your chapter.

The marketplace is waiting. Your community is watching. Your family is following. Will you choose to lead like Jesus?

Devotional Prayer

Father in Heaven, I thank You for the gift of leadership displayed perfectly in Jesus Christ. Thank You for His clarity of identity, His wisdom in timing, His power in storytelling, His excellence in execution, His loyalty through relationship, and His preparation for legacy.

Lord, I confess that I cannot lead well on my own. Pride, fear, and distraction often cloud my vision. But today, I surrender my leadership to You. Teach me to lead like Jesus—with humility, courage, integrity, and love. May my identity be rooted in You. May my vision reflect Your Kingdom. May my actions serve people faithfully. May my legacy point others to Christ.

I ask for wisdom to discern the right timing, discipline to execute with excellence, compassion to build loyalty, and courage to prepare others for leadership. Help me not chase crowds but invest in disciples. Help me not pursue popularity but build legacy. Help me not only succeed but also be significant for Your glory.

Empower me by Your Spirit, Lord, to lead in the marketplace, in my community, and in my home with the values of Jesus.

May those I lead see Him in me. May the culture I build honor You. And may the legacy I leave reflect the One who gave His life for me.

I commit my leadership, my work, and my future into Your hands. In the name of Jesus Christ, the greatest leader and Savior of the world, I pray. Amen.